W9-BGB-356

Cash From Your Garden

Roadside Farm Stands

David W. Lynch

GARDEN WAY PUBLISHING
CHARLOTTE, VERMONT 05445

Printed in the United States by Essex Publishing Company.

Library of Congress catalog card number: 74-75464

International standard book number: 0-88266-056-X (pbk)

Contents

Preface

Before the book now in your hands was published, the only full-length work on the subject was a helpful, now out-of-print 1965 publication by the University of Delaware Press, *Roadside Farm Marketing in the United States.* Compiled by James J. Milmoe from statistical studies done earlier, it served me as a framework of ideas on which to construct a book offering information to help people in the business or thinking of going into it.

My thanks to the University of Delaware Press and the author for approving our use of that publication in creating this book.

I am also indebted to the many extension services and their specialists, who generously supplied me with their ideas, newsletters, and booklets. I would particularly like to thank Roger Ginder, Ransom Blakeley, R. Alden Miller, Lou Albano, and M. E. Cravens, whose ideas have contributed much to the chapters that follow. Their publications and others are listed in detail in the Appendix (p. 200).

Finally, my thanks go to Bruce B. Butterfield for true Vermont kindness, to the editors at Garden Way for competence, and in particular to Walter Hard, Jr., for his patience.

DAVID W. LYNCH
Manchester by the Sea,
Massachusetts

Chapter 1

Why Sell at the Edge of the Road?

COME TO THE COUNTRY
AND SEE

Many of us dream in our youth, and later, too, about running our own business, responsible to no one but ourselves. If we do start to grow crops for sale, it is soon clear that farming can be a good way to make a living. But it's one thing to make hard-worked acres pay by producing all the land will give, and selling it to ever-hungry wholesalers or retailers for smallish profit. Selling directly to the public is another kind of challenge. You have to sell the world, customer by customer, on the merits of your produce, and use your powers of persuasion; you don't simply deliver the merchandise and collect the money. Yet the public can put profit in your pocket *if* you get to know people and handle them gingerly.

One heartwarming reason for putting your wares before the people in your own market is that every unit sold this way brings in more profit than it will if sold to a wholesaler or retailer. You aren't working for someone who will take his own cut of the proceeds on top of money you spent on handling and transportation. The customer will do most of the shipping—at his expense, not yours. Helpful soul, he even does part of your selling job simply by choosing to stop at *your* market, not the one your friend runs down the road. Packing and container costs drop away, too, if you do business hand to hand. All you need to be a marketer is the *time,* the *place* to sell in, and the *effort* of offering the people something they usually want anyway.

It's an easy business to get started in, unlike many others I can think of—or would you prefer to drum up the few hundred thousand that it would take to start big, and compete directly with the chain stores? Most growers start with modest ambitions and turn away from a big, complex, expensive and risky operation. Roadside marketing is a pretty reasonable alternative to supermarketing.

But, we'll pardon you for asking, then what will come of the gardening revolution that we see all around us? People are cultivating their own back yards—even those formerly useless front yards. They're doing away with the lawn and are machine-tilling the soil and making their own compost and using it. Their homes are surrounded by edible crops, grown with energy if not efficiency.

I believe that the revolution will stay with us, that Americans really think about going back to nature's ways and nature's fruits. It's happening only in a small way to most people, but how else would we have it?

SELLING SURPLUS

What about the gardener who cultivates every inch of soil to produce as much as the family can eat? What if he ends up with extra food that is so good it would be a shame to toss it on the compost heap? There is just too much to give away to neighbors who can't bear the sight of another summer squash. What hope can we hold out for a very small grower of produce who has bigger things in mind? Can you make a little money by selling surplus from your garden?

Where is the boundary between harvesting enough for the family, plus preserves to last the winter, and growing more—so much more that you can go beyond the garden surplus and make a profit? I don't know, and I doubt that anyone can give you much of an answer—you have to try to find it. To make a profit, or just to break even, may be a pretty big goal. The cost of cultivation and seed and fertilizer and fighting off insects and disease may not be your biggest problem. Just making back the costs of gardening may mean you can ignore the complications you'll read of in this book.

But realize that to *make a living,* or part of one, by growing and selling your own produce means being businesslike about the whole thing. And that raises the first of our questions: *Do you have the land to produce enough food to stock a little market for more than a couple of weeks? Or do you have the capital to buy produce from competent growers nearby who don't sell directly to the public?* These are just the simplest questions, of course, but they must be answered before you think of depending on income from a little produce sold at a tiny market.

With good luck and a large surplus beyond what you need, you can draw in extra cash in the pleasant way (if the law allows you to sell where you plan to). With a small piece of land, expect to cultivate intensively. You'll have to concentrate on a few varieties, probably, because you won't have the resources to diversify right away. You'll do best with varieties that mature early in the season and also give you a crop late in the season. Succession planting is one way of getting a constant flow of crops into the market. Time your plantings of each crop so that one will be ready to harvest when the one before it gives out. That takes extra land, clearly. Interplanting is another possibility. Plant root crops *between* widely spaced vine crops, or other combinations. But then watch out at harvest time. A job that has to be done quickly and accurately may become difficult if the harvest is large and has to be gotten to in a hurry to prevent spoilage.

As you'll see later on, most farm marketers grow half or more of their own produce. But, to make a small start, nothing says that you can't set up an arrangement with other local gardeners to buy their surplus and sell it at your market. To make this arrangement and supply your market with enough variety and quantity may take the capacity of a computer and a degree from a business school—but you might be the one to get it working. You could buy surplus from local farmers as long as they are willing to give you the best of their crop, not inferior grades.

My answer to these questions then is this: you can get a start if you don't count on earning a big income immediately. Read this book to be aware of what you'll need to know when you do make a business of growing and selling directly to the public. And think of my suggestions as possible solutions to future problems, and to present problems on a small scale. Always, always be open to ideas from any source— a book, an article, other growers and marketers, even other businesses—which may help you improve the service you provide your customers. It may mean no great blooming of profits right away, but invest in good will, because that brings and keeps customers.

SMALL CAPITAL, LOW RISK

The capital outlay for a market can be small; you don't have to sell by the hundreds of tons to make a profit. Of course if you prefer to dream about those big but chancy profits and you think high-pressure business is good for the health, you could always sink $100,000 to a quarter of a million into a doughnut or hamburg or chicken or other franchise. Profits there are unbelievably big, and so are the doctor's bills. You might make back your investment in a year, but if it costs you

ten years of life, it just might not be worth it. Roadside
marketing, on the other hand—if you go about it in a
reasonable way at the beginning—doesn't expose you or
your creditors to any great risk. Even if terrible crop years
hurt both the producing and selling ends of your business, in
this kind of work you're not dealing in millions, so that
disaster insurance is just about built in.

As a proprietor, you answer to no boss but the American
public, the competition and your own ambitious impulses.
All three can be brutal taskmasters, but you've put yourself
in charge of the planning and imagination departments and
that means you're in control. Planning, thinking, and plain
hard work can bring satisfaction to both sides of the
counter—to you and to the buying public.

Then too, living where your business is will be one of the
most satisfying parts of direct marketing. As a current or a
potential grower you probably know that country life, in
spite of its tough side, is likable. Try living and working in
the city for a while and see the difference that country living
and working makes in your life.

This is a seasonal business for many marketers. You can
use that limitation for your own advantage by doing something else that interests you during the off season. Or you can
ignore nature's restrictions and handle products that you
can grow and sell in all seasons, simply by expanding your
facilities. We'll look at that possibility later.

If you choose total independence, you can do all your own
growing or producing. Middlemen will be no part of your life.
The share of the profits they might swallow can stay home to
build your own fortune. And some ways of supplementing
your production can be worked into the overall plan to keep
the costs down while the profits grow healthy. Being your
own supplier, you can cut out the purchasing burden that for
other producers is a big one, absorbing time, patience, and
capital.

Some people find that a producing business can get shaky
because taxes inflate as the value of land goes up, threatening to drive them off the land and into urban living. Many of
these producers welcome the chance to increase profits by
retail selling.

With a roadside business, overhead can be nearly as low as you decide to make it. Sell only your own produce at your own stand on land that you own already. For the really fortunate marketer all the staff that's needed is his own family. That reduces the salary drain and the bookkeeping, and it can guarantee high-quality help. Seeing the family business working efficiently and prospering is all the incentive your relatives may need to put out a quantity and quality of work seldom purchasable from hired help. Every effort they make has a good chance of bettering everyone's life; in other words, the family that works together prospers together.

WHAT'S IN IT FOR THE PAYING CUSTOMER?

Now, if these benefits are on your side of the ledger, how do you get Mr. and Mrs. Public to see the good things in this deal for them? Just make it clear that they can't find any vegetables and fruits fresher, purer and of higher quality than you offer. The consumers will soon prove to you that a lot of people believe in freshness and quality, even at an undiscounted price. They get full value for their money, more than anywhere else but their own gardens (if they are so equipped) or from other roadside markets. With an efficient operation you may even give them food at prices a shade lower than they will find at most other retail stores.

It may be easier for many people to get to your place of business than, say, to a city supermarket. Getting there adds to the fun, too, if your place is a little way out in that magical place there isn't much left of—the country. Rural surroundings and farm atmosphere have a drawing power. Besides, farm people who tend markets are real human beings, warm and friendly most of the time, unlike big-store automatons working thanklessly for huge corporations.

The country has advantages you can make hay on. Another ally for the marketer is the great American four-wheeled crutch, the car. It's the city and suburb dweller's escape machine, ready any time to carry the family beyond the endless concrete walls and subdivisions into the farmland where good things can be seen, heard and bought. Expensive gasoline and tight money don't seem reason enough to stay home if you can make a useful *and* scenic trip for good produce. The newspapers say that more cars are on the road than ever, though the trips people take may be shorter than they used to be. They're willing to drive far enough to reach the markets they know.

IS THIS THE WORK FOR YOU?

Now, a few questions that you can ask yourself to see if this is the business for you.

First, is roadside marketing the best way to sell your produce? You'll have to figure out all the costs, savings and profits, of course. The reason for going into business is fully or partly to support yourself and family, which means taking some risk. Figure this risk in with your projected costs, and see if you can afford to lose your investment if luck should take a bad turn. Then decide if, in this short and risky life, it's worth stretching your neck for something worthwhile. Then go to the bank.

Knowing how much you do produce and estimating how much more you could grow if you had to, figure roughly how before and after would work out at wholesale and retail prices. I'll try to give you some help on those later on. Does the final figure look like nothing more than a meager supplementary income? Then a very small, part-time operation, taking little volume away from your other kinds of selling, is probably the way to go. If your figurings show any promise of an *increase* in your income coming from retail sales, then ask yourself if you have the time to put into this part of the business. Lots of farmers hesitate to invest the kind of time roadside marketing takes, because their profits from selling to retailers and wholesalers haven't been *that* bad.

And besides, long-time producers may think being a salesman and having to please the fickle public is a nuisance. After all, producers are getting scarcer every year. The land brings high prices from speculators or developers—anyone who can round up the cash and not have to stop eating until the speculation pays off. Every sale of farmland to a developer and every developer's sale of a house or business lot to a buyer is reflected in land values and then in taxes, except in some enlightened states that tax land by its *current* use, not its potential (developed) market value. All this has driven some farmers to the ragged edge of nerves and finances. All they can do is sell out or find money in some other way.

The only good in this tragedy is that with so many pulling out of the food-producing business, driven away by high taxes, low prices, high costs, or simply old age, fewer people are left to do the job. This exodus unfortunately adds to the trend toward agribusiness, which might seem the only way left to make big money in producing. But these continuing surrenders also cut the number of smaller farmers and marketers. Fewer are left to feed more and more consumers. Opportunity in roadside marketing, always big, is likely to keep expanding. Close-in farmlands in metropolitan areas of course may have reached saturation, with too many markets crammed into their parts of the country. Yet even in these places comings and goings of markets are constant; possibilities are opening all the time, to be cut off only when the life of the land is killed forever.

Chapter 2

Starting Out

People who run their markets for the shortest possible seasons may not come near making a living from them, but M. E. Cravens tells us that when you add it all together, the business these part-time marketers do may be greater than that done by the regular farm retail markets in his home state, Ohio. Some of them do not have a regular market. They may be berry growers, farmers with a few fruit trees or some sweet corn, tomatoes or beans, and livestock or poultry producers who sell a little meat or eggs at retail.

To keep your risks low and your capital under the mattress, you can manage nearly a riskless start by testing the market for potential customers with small beginnings. It does take more than a back-yard garden, but not much more. Once you feel some ground under foot, it will be time enough to think bigger.

HOW MUCH INCOME DO YOU WANT?

You'll quickly notice that the markets I talk about throughout this book are somewhat bigger than the old-kitchen-table-under-the-maple variety. My reason for spending most time on the moderate-sized, family-operated business is clear enough, and I'll say it simply: It's a matter of making a living.

Many people would love to produce and sell just a little more than they're doing with their back-yard garden plot. They now have a little surplus to give away or sell. But must they expand greatly to prosper a little?

Perhaps not. With a garden big by city standards but small for rural areas, carefully tended, immensely fertile, they could follow hints like those offered on "Crockett's Victory Garden" and squeeze some supplementary "profits" from their garden.

That's not making a living, though. To make a living at it, you'll need: (1) a couple of acres, at least, (2) a small investment in machinery, (3) shelters for equipment and market, and (4) perhaps extra capital to cover supplementary purchases from local farms.

Starting small—maybe with a garden big enough just for your own needs—you may discover that you love growing produce and like the idea of selling it for a plumper income. You're ready to plow under the hobby garden and get serious about growing to sell.

Be thoughtful, though. Move gradually. Growth must come first in your supply of produce. Will you grow more crops or purchase more? Increased production means learning how much of what to plant, and how to grow it for the biggest possible yield—very simply, how to manage bigger and perhaps different crops.

How you increase production is an area I must reluctantly skip over, though it is important to the whole picture. Here we must concentrate on marketing alone.

Once you do have more produce to sell, however, direct marketing with a roadside stand can bring you a second income—or even your main supply of cash. We can't ignore, either, that the joy of gardening is a plural pleasure, giving many kinds of profit, no matter what the garden's size. One of these profits can be financial.

But heed my warning, repeated several times through these pages: It is no small step from a little home garden—supplying the family with fresh and canning foods—to real food production and big, salable crops. The leap to a home-grown income you can live on is not to be made without cautious measuring.

Let's say you've arrived at one of the three possibilities for fattening such income: adding acreage, increasing productivity, or finding a sound local source to buy produce from. You might now stop and think about the troubles and consequences of metamorphosing from a little producer-marketer to a bigger one. The challenges are not minor, yet they are truly threatening only when ignored. As we go on into the subject, I hope to bring these factors out where we can see them and learn how to solve them.

The heaviest difficulty stands out already. If you do work up a fair-sized producing and marketing business, how can one mere human (namely you) handle two businesses at once?

With luck, your spouse or someone else in the family may

be the one to take over the side of the business you don't care to run yourself. Two able managers in one family running their own specialties can make a potent business.

Things can happen, of course, to every fine arrangement. Children may come along, swallowing so much time one parent has to drop out for a while. Grown young people may not choose to stay with the business. The farming-marketing families I've seen have held together because there's enough to keep all of them interested, busy and financially comfortable—though not fat. Many also are families that have lived and worked in close harmony. And they all worked like hell.

A business that grows beyond the size that family managers can handle demands an urgent solution. Then, too, some people just don't care to be managers or lack the talent. Be ready to find a manager if or when the business cries out for one.

My suggestions then are: (1) Start small, grow gradually to keep planning several steps ahead of necessity. (2) Get the family in on the project and keep them there with all the incentives you can give—cheerful managing, careful sharing of the work and the rewards. (3) Know about the local labor market into which you may have to dip for help.

IMMEDIATE QUESTIONS

Time.   Let's say that you already have the land, that the producing part of your business is taking care of itself without your close attention, and that you intend to start a market. You may have to figure, during your first season anyhow, on giving the market all your time. That's operating time—60 to 70 hours a week in the most active part of the season isn't unusual. And that counts no time for paper work and planning, unless you can keep those going during selling hours (which is a good idea, by the way). You do have to be on hand when people are there to buy—nights perhaps, weekends and holidays certainly. Still, with health, patience and energy, time should be the least worrisome of your limitations.

Capital. Next, can you get your hands on enough capital to make your start promising, no matter how small? Will the family savings stand such a bite? Will your friend the banker, who should be in on the planning with you from the beginning, be able to arrange a loan that won't put too much strain on your cash flow? Even for the smallest market (if you intend to make a real business of it) building, equipment, supplies, and maybe salaries have to be worked in.

Location. Is your location practical for a market that depends on people getting to you easily, on a road with adequate traffic, for enough people to give you a steady patronage?

Quantity. Can you arrange regular harvests, with the crops ripening in sequence all through the season so that at all times you'll have enough to sell and enough variety of produce to attract the one-stop shoppers who would like to buy almost everything they need at one place? Or do you know of a reliable source for extra produce, perhaps neighboring farmers who have surplus and other crops and might be willing to reduce their price for quantity sales to you?

Staff. Can your family alone staff the business, or will you have to go after less dependable, more expensive outside help?

The public. Finally, do you think that you can handle the public, a demanding but rewarding audience?

If you can confidently say yes to these questions, you may find yourself ready to start in one of the oldest and surest businesses, and to make a living at it. All you need is to spend several hours of heavy thought, a few more in exact planning, and then to ask yourself questions (I've phrased as many as I could for you in these pages), and to get answers from the right people.

WHAT ARE THE PROBLEMS?

The public heads the list of those you will be responsible to when you run a successful food-selling business. You are in business to serve them. You do have to let them know you're there, with advertising in kinds and amounts you pick. Everything you do to attract them, from the signs you put by the roadside to the advertising space you buy, has to put out a strong, consistent image of your superior produce and your ability as a marketer.

Quality, as people serious about roadside marketing agree, is one of the great selling points farm markets have. Customers getting the fruits and vegetables directly from the one who produced them expect a lot. They want to believe the individual seller cares that the merchandise is the best—free of defects in appearance, not poisoned with pesticides or crawling with bugs, at its ripened peak, fresh out of the ground or off the vine or tree, grown with care and handled as though it were the customer's property.

Service is a product, and its quality counts at least as much as that of your produce. Some people who farm successfully for years and then go into selling by the road's edge have trouble adjusting their attitudes. It's as if they thought "growing is my real work; I'm not a salesman. Let the customers sell themselves. Besides, the produce is its own best salesman." When you've dealt with the public for a while you find out how tough it is to get a customer, how big a job it can be to keep people happy with your market. Going out of your way pays more than extra profits—it's the debt you owe the people who pay your way by buying what you make.

You have a great advantage as a producer because you are selling the things your ability has brought to fruition. The more a salesman knows about his product and how it was made, the more he can say about it. Think how few of the salesmen you've met know more about their product than the words memorized from their company's sales manual. Too many get a surface knowledge and can answer only the everyday questions. Give them a tough one and they may not even know where to start looking for the answer. But you have all the information about your merchandise. Try to feel the moment when the shopper will appreciate a *little* extra knowledge. Very few will stand still as you tell them everything they didn't need to know about how you grow a radish. Service means offering a good product, helpful salesmanship, a neat, attractive package, and a nice-looking market.

One of the easier parts of dealing with the public, I've heard people say, is keeping them friendly. Not true, except perhaps for someone who has a boisterously outgoing personality. Having a friendly customer takes more than just being friendly yourself. That's only half the recipe. The public has as many moods and attitudes as it has heads. Maybe a third of the people you meet in a day are so tight in their shells that making your way in would be like cracking a skull. They don't need to be friendly and for that reason alone some of them aren't. Of course, that doesn't mean you should be cold in return. A professional's secure feeling about the quality of the merchandise should keep you calm and above most troublesome moments. Even if nearly all your customers are local regulars, you'll get an occasional neighborhood crab or transient grouser who's ready to snap at you before, during, and after you've sold her or him something, or even if he has bought nothing at all. Pleasing him while making a little money is an accomplishment to be glad about. It's worth the effort though it may give you a pain in the inside. Make friends!

Your responsibility. Feel your responsibility to yourself and your family. As a grower you might shy away from adding this new burden, but it can bring security and a better way of life, and you can set a fine example for children by working hard and successfully with them at your side. To live up to your duty you'll have to do a thorough job on your marketing; you can't stand still. Keep learning from everything you can get your hands on about marketing. Go around to nearby markets to see how others do business. It may take several visits to spot differences between your market and the one on the other side of town. Talk with the owners and with your county agent and people at the extension services. List your questions so that you'll have them handy when you talk to the one who may have the answer. Get as many answers as you can *before* the problems come up. Watch for meetings of marketers from other parts of your state and out of state too. These get-togethers encourage people in the business to do all they can to keep roadside marketing a healthy part of a state's food industry.

Plan constantly. Even if it seems impractical, spend time daydreaming and scheming for the future of your market. Making the business grow is just part of this responsibility; in your market, as in any business, growth isn't always the best prescription. Look ahead for anything that you can improve: changing displays, advertising more, or doing it more effectively; handling cash more shrewdly; trying other ways of selling; selling new items; even building a whole new market. Think steadily about these possibilities and stay ahead of the future.

Being businesslike and professional about everything in your business isn't just a matter of keeping busy or even of watching everything that's going on in your own place or in markets around you. Knowing your produce is part of this attitude, and you'll have to be knowledgeable about all kinds of ways in which people can use the foods you sell. Mostly, professionalism in marketing means knowing what's going on and why things are done as they are.

Small but good. You ought to be able to answer every question anyone might ask when they look at your ways of doing business—why you charge this price for one quantity and that price for another. Is everything you do each day in the market the most efficient (not the easiest) way of doing it? Are you or is anyone else in the market really good at doing what you and they are doing right now and every day?

Roadside marketing is thought of as a coming business. Scholarly papers are being written on many things about the business, as experts look at what makes it go and think about how it could go better. Let's hope it won't ever be inflated into another multi-billion-dollar monstrosity like the one the old-fashioned grocery store turned into. But neither is it going to wither and float away on a midsummer breeze.

CHALLENGE FROM OUTSIDE— THE COMPETITION

Indirect competitors can steal attention from you. Though a market may be off in the sticks, it is never far from some kind of business that is competing for the public's attention. By competition I mean anything that might keep people from seeing your signs or market or advertising or produce, or from paying enough attention to these to make your efforts worthwhile. With the market on a road carrying much traffic, you're in luck if it's not surrounded by retailers of everything on earth. "Convenience" stores are there (some of them handling produce) staying open to grab customers at all hours; chain supermarkets with their variety of merchandise, their tiny margin of profit but huge volume; shopping "mall" collections of every kind of retailer, from big, high-priced stores to cheapies selling junk; food servers with specialized restaurants, lucrative pizza, hamburg, pancake, and doughnut joints greasing the public palate. All of them—chained, franchised or independent—are competing for the same customers' eyes and mouths. Even the billboards, if your state allows them, are competing with you.

Your direct competition. Nearby, along with this assorted company, may be other marketers like yourself. Some may have small but healthy markets run by conscientious growers who produce most of their own goods carefully and sell them honestly. Not far away, you might run into small or middlesized operators who, whether or not they grow their own, have lower standards and don't do quite so good a job. Their reputations spread quickly; you'll soon know which to watch. Then there are some of larger size, more or less commercial marketers who buy more than half of their merchandise. Depending on their taste, these can be strong, likable neighbors or shoddy peddlers of low-quality merchandise. They can also attract people, transients or locals, and intentionally or not, sell them non-native produce for the real thing. All they need is enough people out for a ride who happen in to buy something. Some city dwellers won't even know the difference between freshly harvested and shipped-in food—for a while. Eventually though, they'll go looking for something better, and if it happens to be at your market, they might learn a lesson: some markets do sell excellent local produce.

Then you'll probably find not far off the used-to-be-small roadside market that is turning into a supermarket. It can be recognized by its can't-be-missed blazing sign, shilling people into a glass-fronted, warehouse-like cinder-block building; squatting on an acre of blacktop. And the parking lot is as likely as not to be cramful of cars, many from out of state.

LEARN FROM THEIR ERRORS

How can you use the competition without joining them? Instead of thinking unhappy thoughts about some of these fellow merchants, learn from them. If you don't go too far with it, this way of getting knowledge substitutes in a small way for real experience. Look at their selling techniques, store layouts, effective or garish displays, the prices they charge for things you sell too, checkout arrangements, packaging, parking, equipment, attractiveness—everything they have and all they do.

Competitors do you one big service, gratis, by drawing possible customers to the countryside where you also do business. Exposure to more people can't hurt, especially if by alert merchandising you can convert some of them into friends of your market. This is the big advantage if your market is small, personal, friendly, attractive and full of excellent merchandise. Make your special advertising and selling image as a small, high-quality source of good food just as strong as truth can paint it. Profit by your advantages, because these are the competition's weaknesses. And remember that repeat customers are your first goal—your most reliable profits are mostly in the hands of the local people to whom you make yourself known. Naturalness in appearance and produce should bring in the kind of customer who doesn't care for mass-produced stuff promoted by all kinds of frippery. Getting across these priceless strengths is the sign of an able marketer.

CHANGE BY THE ROADSIDE:
IS MARKETING HARDER
NOW?

Where are the people? We could go to demographers to find out how fast the landscape is changing from farmlands to car-and-people-filled cityscapes. Of course we don't need statistics to know how different the American scene has become in a few years. In some places only small differences in tawdriness show where one housing tract starts and another burgeons noisily. The farms are now far from most metropolitan places. A few small holdings are still worked, but many of those await the bulldozers. Nearly everyone in the crowded places is fed now by the faraway agribusinesses. Consumers learn little about food fresh from the land as the farm industry works its miracles unseen by most. Yet each farmer who sells his land opens a bit more opportunity for the growers who keep at it; a little less fresh local produce is available to the public. If he was a retailer, his customers will feel the loss and go looking for another retailing producer.

This sad change at least can be on your side if you had the foresight to stay in the business or to be starting out just now. But you'll have to stretch your neck to get these people to come to you. As farms go into nothingness and people spread over the land, they do at least settle closer to the farms that are left. That is bad for the countryside but it does mean that instead of having to drive many miles from city or suburb to the country, they're almost there without leaving home. In the many overpopulous places that means your potential audience has grown without any effort by you to build it; all you do is have enough produce to sell when purchasers come to your doorstep.

Transportation as well as population has changed the retail marketer's life. Wholesalers used to have to spend plenty to bring in the produce, and charge high prices to the retailers they supplied. Time and geography were against them, because they had to ship by slow transportation to their buyers a whole country away. The local retailer had one great advantage. He had freshly grown produce with no shipping or wholesale charges to pass on to the consumer.

Produce aplenty has Mr. Brigante in his crop-surrounded market in Colchester, Vermont. The foods are within reach, grouped by colors for varied display, and prices are visible. No fripperies in this family-run market, just good native foods.

When you have a stand in the fields, why be pretentious? And Sonny says it's good eating.

That stuff from far away, no longer fresh and high priced in spite of mass production, could not compete after being on the road for a week or more—it simply wasn't alive. Now, transportation has cheapened, with railroads, trucks, piggybacks and even air freight competing for longhaul loads. The imported produce *is* a competitive commodity. Yet it still can't beat the freshly harvested, tree- or vine-ripened produce. Selling directly to the public, you're not taking on the whole rest of the country.

SHORTAGES: ANOTHER PROBLEM

Scarce money and expensive energy, unemployment, restricted travel, and some years, on top of it all, miserable growing weather—all mean only one thing: Marketers must do harder thinking, planning and working. You might have to add products, grow more and different varieties, stretch the selling season, or spend more on advertising to reach for more distant customers. But people aren't going to be kept away from fresh food just because of costly gasoline. Even if the financial climate is unhealthy, they still have to eat. And they can find better food for no more—or even for less—at local roadside markets. Bad weather for growing can hurt terribly; so take a step toward beating that problem by diversifying the weatherproof products, which I'll go into.

One of the more threatening ideas I've seen is the starting of *chain* roadside markets. That seems to be a self-defeating proposition. Who knows, though? It could be a way of keeping farms alive, of stopping agricultural land from being covered with houses, roads and industries.

THE MEDIA HELP

Factors balancing some of these large problems may be the gardening revolution and the popular and effective cooking programs being broadcast on the public television channels. Julia Child (French chef) and Joyce Chen (Chinese cooking) are telling people how vital fresh vegetables and fruits are to gourmet eating. Crockett's Victory Garden has been showing people how to grow their own vegetables, a first step in getting them to go out after the good things you have to offer. Thalassa Cruso, talking of *Making Things Grow,* has been doing the same for people who sell plants.

Gene Logsdon in *Organic Gardening and Farming,* August, 1973, has useful ideas on how to beat the big and small competition. He says grow the produce that machines can't help with, such as asparagus and sweet corn, because buying it out of the field is the only way to get it while it tastes good. Big dessert strawberries don't ship well but they sell wildly to roadside and local market customers. And southern growers, who corner the early season market with some items, can't do it with raspberries because these too ship badly; no practical machines have been invented for picking them and you can't pick them when they're green. Logsdon also suggests muskmelons and big, juicy varieties of tomatoes that don't travel well and must be picked by hand. Pole beans are better than the ordinary machine-pickable snap beans. Try pears instead of the apples everyone grows, eggplants instead of the cucumbers that are so easy to grow in large quantities. The good but hard-to-grow kinds of squash like Golden Nugget, with other specialties, may put you ahead of competing roadside marketers.

A CHECKLIST FOR STARTING CONDITIONS

Whether you're in the roadside market business already or are getting ready to start up, think again about these necessities before moving ahead:

(1) The location you settle on has to have something outstanding to recommend it. If you have no choice and must start far off the traveled highway, don't stop planning. Think even harder about how you can attract more people. Or rent space for the market on someone else's farm, at the best rate you can haggle.

(2) Allow for a reasonable amount of expense for maintenance, a little more becoming necessary each year.

(3) Plan a neat, good-looking, but *not* gaudy layout. Invest enough in your start and the costs will be lower later.

(4) Make the parking area as safe as common sense allows, easy enough for the dumbest driver to get into, around and out of without sawing at the steering wheel.

(5) If you put together a comprehensive plan for ads and signs and figure out an advertising budget, half the worry about getting and keeping customers will vanish. Displays, fancy or simple, have to be worked out long in advance of your opening, first year and every year.

(6) Uncompromising quality will cost more in hours of labor and supplies, but it's such a vital part of any market's goodwill that you can't afford to plan without it. If you expect from the beginning to give big quantities in your packaging, customers will notice it, and there's the start of a loyal clientele.

(7) Then, when you have allowed for all the rest, add a big measure of courteous, friendly, helpful service for everyone who comes by, whether they look as if they'll buy or not. This is no place for grouches, early in the morning, late at night, or ever.

Chapter 3

Planning the Market

Once you have thought about the countless problems and possible solutions, the pluses and minuses that can't be separated from selling by the edge of the road, clear your mental drawing board so that your next step, planning, can be put together timber by timber. Getting a business going, even a small one, is not done without a plan. Decide that you want to get into roadside selling and then spend plenty of hours on the big question: how? Even if you're busy producing all day, the planning has to be done, and you'll probably have to find hours in the evening to sit and to think—on paper. Black and white planning at the start can save you many later stumbles.

WHERE TO START

What are your goals? About the earliest thinking you'll get to is deciding exactly what your goals will be. Assemble these, from the first day of the season all the way through closing day (if you plan an end-of-season shutdown). Put every goal on paper and it will make a handy checklist as you move along, reminding you where you should be *now* and warning you when action will be needed to get you where you should be week by week. No wishes or hopes can sneak into this goal-thinking. Just clear, definite, straightforward, verifiable objectives will appear here.

What is possible? That's half the guidance you need in planning realistically. The other half is just as useful—what *can't* be done? You ought to know your physical, financial, productive and competitive limitations. Start off by thinking big, being a total optimist about your plan. How big could the business be if you threw everything into it, even if it meant risking everything you own? Be the biggest market in the county, selling everything you can grow and more besides.

Then try putting the brakes on imagination and take the pessimistic way of looking at your possibilities. What is the smallest building, the most limited number of customers and the smallest volume of sales you might be unfortunate enough to build up? What would the worst that bad weather two or more years in a row, the foulest depression, the most painfully pinching shortages of gasoline or artificial fertilizer (if you use it), or anything else do to your business? Now you have your most spacious and your tightest boundaries drawn around the possibilities. Build for a future somewhere between the extremes.

With these goals well in mind, you can start adjusting your tools for reaching them by looking closely at the reality. How well off are you in land, capital, and management? Will these resources get you where you want to go in business? Match up goals and resources carefully: cash and credit with building and equipment, projected income with operating cost, planned acreage in crops for each season with the volume of goods you'd like to see, and the possible size of your audience with the length of your season, for both growing and selling.

What's your minimum? If you can't get just the kind or size of market that seems right, have another plan to fall back on. When you get down to serious talk with bankers, insurance agents, suppliers, agricultural agents and other helpful people and find that your hopes were bigger than your crops, this contingency plan might take you in an even more profitable, though different, direction. If your acreage should turn out to be too small to support a full-time market, just figure how much you'd need to earn from a part-time business to keep you going until you have money enough to build your holdings. Or you could go into a wholly nonproducing business, selling only produce grown by other people. Big incomes are made in that way — but it would take another book to handle the subject.

When will you accomplish the things you have to do to get going? Be realistic. Plan only as much size and volume as your resources can easily handle in the first year. You can be more expansive in planning later years; the only punishment for dreaming ahead is disappointment. But write out your schedule to know what should happen, and when.

The idea behind all this planning is that if you can foresee troubles that *could* come, you'll at least have a start at settling them. At the height of your rush season (let's assume you'll have a rush season) you might find something wasn't planned all the way through. Flow of traffic in and out of the parking area may be frustratingly slow or people could be wasting time in unprofitable parts of your market, not traveling swiftly from display to checkout. That's an awful time to have to stop for snappy managerial decision-making. Plan now, cover everything, both the big and the small goings-on in your future market. It saves later sweat.

Now, in whatever order you think is practical, plan the kind of market that's right for your resources. Are you prepared to handle a big, country-style supermarket (if you could invent such an incongruous combination). Can you manage and will your area support a market carrying hundreds of items? Or is a lean-to attached to the barn more within reach, presenting some or all of the crops you grow, but nothing from outside your own fields? Which kind of market will best serve the customers you expect to go after? Spell out the major and minor limits of the market's size and your ambition before you reach for that hammer.

Consider alternatives. What are some of the choices marketers try when they find that selling their own crops doesn't give the profits they feel are needed? Some farmers have tried door-to-door selling — they need very strong stomachs for all the *No*s they are bound to get. Some selling may still be done in that way. But I think it might be wearisome and inefficient to drive around all day, more pleasant to stay with the farm and the market, keeping both under your eye.

What about adding a pick-it-yourself operation to the market? That can be a way to add two skins to the barn door. The customers do the harvesting and you get the profits. You can attract people who might not otherwise come to the market, thinking your prices too high for them. Run the pickers past your market on the way in and out, have things priced as they want to see them, and put the prices up where they will see them clearly. Read more about this subject in Chapter 9. Try direct deliveries to local supermarkets or other retail outlets, if you can build some business there. Truck farming flourishes in many places.

A side business? A side business tied to a market on the farm can keep you going until (if you want it to) the market can stand by itself. And such a business can take the pressure off the market. With one of these selling ways going strong you can adjust the market's size as you get ready to. Many people have started out selling by a busy highway off the back of a truck or from a trailer or a farm wagon or just a table or two out by the farmhouse. In a little while these are likely to be less than satisfying, because they attract few people and little profit—usually. Having a bigger spread seems to bring customers expecting more variety and willing to spend a little more for larger quantities of good food. The typical successful marketer, though, grows more than half the produce sold, and sells it on or near his farm, hires some outside help, works in a simple market building in an attractive farm setting, caters to local repeat customers, and gets little income from the transient trade running past the door. He deals directly with the public for three to six months of the year.

Even in the mostly rural states like North Dakota, farm management economist Tom Reff tells me, the ones with many huge farms, few big cities, and not much of an audience for roadside marketers to take advantage of, a few farmers do make a little extra by selling sweet corn and potatoes. Some also sell milk or eggs to regular customers. But that is more like farm or garden surplus than roadside marketing.

Commercial markets. If you are able to start off with the kind of market we can call commercial or semi-commercial you will have less to worry about than the fellow with the tiny farm stand, though you take on extra problems the smaller marketers don't have to think about. With this kind of business you would grow less than half of the produce you sold. You might, like many others who have markets of this size, be close to a large city, where land is dear but transportation isn't. Here, you can be reached quickly by city dwellers and their ample wallets. Here too, though, the competition from all kinds of retailers is more direct and can be ferocious.

What to sell at the market? Healthy variety. More than anything else food shoppers come to the country to pick up many kinds of fruit and vegetables that are as fresh, attractive and inexpensive as you can serve up. The more variety you have waiting for them, the bigger their average purchases will be. More kinds of produce also mean more and better-looking displays, which, if luck, advertising, and weather support you, may draw good-sized crowds. That people like to get all their fresh produce at one place is an old truism. But even though you carry all the vegetables and some of the fruits and berries liked by people where you live, it's almost impossible to plan to have all their shopping items ready for them. The long wait for fruit trees to start bearing is one unsolvable problem when you're starting out. Some sellers start with all vegetables, which is fair enough because most health-conscious households try to get plenty of those during the fresh season and a few more during the winter in preserved or frozen form. Specializing in fruit is not a bad bet either, because almost everyone likes it and believes in its healthfulness. But climate is an almost sure limiter when you're planning what to grow. Diversify, say with sweet corn, salad makings, and apples, and you should be able to keep people coming through the season.

Be cautious. Marketers starting out are expected to experiment to see what demand will do with a number of items that common sense says should go together well. Yet beginners ought to step cautiously. Maybe just a few of the local favorites will be enough to get you through a season or two, before you build up to a comprehensive, customer-pleasing mixture of produce. As long as everything you grow, at either end of the season or in the middle, is noticeably high in quality, limited variety shouldn't handicap you. Reputations are built by serving up enough good stuff at decent prices—not large numbers of items of imperfect quality and undependable quantity.

Starting small is safest. From one to five kinds of fruits and vegetables may get you under way. When you find you can read the public mind better, after a few seasons, and have enough customers to keep business wholesome, then is the time to branch out, adding items that will appeal to more and more of them.

First in popularity is fruit. Grow some of the favorite kinds and you're bound to find willing customers. Apples, peaches, pears, plums, strawberries, blueberries, raspberries, and blackberries—that's the roster of well-loved fruits. Among the vegetables the top favorites always seem to be sweet corn, tomatoes, beans, potatoes, lettuce and other salad vegetables. M. E. Cravens, professor of agricultural economics and rural sociology at Ohio State University, verifies this order of public preference and grower production. A while back in northeastern Ohio, he writes, apples made up 89 percent of the marketers' sales, followed by 80 percent for peaches and 55 percent for sweet corn. Acreages in fruit, he says, are double those in vegetables. Altogether, those are the crops that sell best fresh and appeal to the local customers. Selling other products gets you into more competition from other sellers where absolute freshness doesn't seem to count so much.

Follow local preferences. Get your guidance in what to grow mostly by reading local preferences and by considering the things it's *possible* for you to grow or to buy for resale. Watch how things sell at local stands. Get hints from your local extension marketer and the other sources we've mentioned. Then it's up to you to bring the people to buy what you offer, adjusting from season to season as you learn their mind.

PLACE THE MARKET WELL

SELL WHERE YOU GROW

No one can say where you will do your most effective selling—in your front yard or miles away on a rented plot. It's clear enough that to get your wares exposed to the best combination of local and fly-by-night customers you should be on a two-lane, not-too-fast road with medium-heavy traffic. At the same time, the great appeal of plunking the market in a field where people can see the fresh and wholesome foods right where they're raised might lead you to choose your own one-lane dirt road (not far from the

highway), where they know they are in producing country. Most people's experiences seem to tell us that a compromise is best. The scattershot method is most useful to the commercial kind of marketer, counting on being spotted by a small but predictable percentage among all the crowds who go by—in other words depending on chance and the fast-moving customer's passing fancy. You may not really want constant, nose-to-tail traffic around your place of business. You also aren't likely to be allowed to set up a business on a limited-access road, and besides, people move too fast there. In the little time they have to notice your market, they may hesitate to stop their rapid progress.

Let's look at the site simply, going over the most desirable qualities a small-to-middling marketer ought to look for. If traffic and accessibility are most important to you, figure out how big a population of potential buyers is within a few miles of you, say five miles at the outside (which is how far many people seem willing to drive). If you don't know how many cars go by on a typical day, your county or town highway department or city planners or department of commerce may be able to help you. Or count them yourself on a busy weekend afternoon. Too much traffic can be worse than too little—people hesitate to cut out of the flow of traffic because it can be hard to stick their noses back in again. And if they are flying by at 55 miles an hour you also may have to sink too much money into signs to drag them off the road.

Let's say you have the first few conditions about right—not too far from consuming civilization, about the right amount of traffic, not an overload of local competition but enough to keep the road traveled much of the time. Then, if you have a choice, pick a flat spot where they will have a clear view of you a fair distance away. Do what you can to keep from limiting the traveler's view of your market. You don't need too many trees, too much setback, thickly parked cars (obscuring your well-built, neatly landscaped frontage), or large signs — which are terrible at drawing the kind of customers you're looking for. On the other hand, if you put everything too close to the road, hoping to get most exposure to the roving public eye, instead your eyes may fill with dust, your lungs with fumes and your ears with road noise. Worse still is an embankment separating you from the road. Only if they can *see* you will they try to get to you.

Put your market in a hilly area, and an uphill climb will slow the cars enough, with the market right at the crest, so that drivers can sight you in time to stop and shop. A curve is usually a difficult place, because it's naturally hard, with short sighting distance, to see your whole layout from a car, evaluate it, slow down, and pull in. A straightaway gives you a sporting chance of catching them if your sign language is well planned. You might want to place the market itself so that it shows off its best side—the front—to the approaching driver. This would cut down on some of the outdoor advertising you might otherwise have to invest in.

Allenholm, run by Ray Allen in South Hero, Vermont. An orchard market with apples of many varieties, free tastes of cider and cheese and ham, and big electric oven home-baked pies. Easy to enter and leave the large, uncluttered parking area.

Having the market fairly close to your house and barn or even attached to them can be helpful, unless you feel that's getting business too close to home. The site does have to be spacious enough for safe parking and possible expansion at some time later on. Put the market at least within convenient distance of the house, storage buildings and the source of supply. It is best to be very near or among the fields you cultivate. A few shade trees among the green fields or orchards are a blessing for making customers comfortable, cooling workers, and keeping produce well-preserved. The right-hand side of the road, headed in toward the nearest town, is a pretty desirable arrangement. Having other businesses nearby on the same road is a good plan, for extra people-drawing attractions.

SELL AT A DISTANCE

But let's say your land doesn't have most of these fine ideals built in. You can always do some looking around for a better spot, and if you're diplomatic and lucky, find the landowner friendly to a businesslike neighbor and not against taking a little income out of a piece of land that may be sitting idle. The big trouble with this absentee marketing (if you grow a lot of your own produce) is that you have to get the produce from one place to the other, and even a short distance can mean more handling, which makes more work and less-than-fresh foods. Think about those inconveniences, plus the clear advantage that having the market flanked by fields and reeking of farm atmosphere can give you if you sell right from the farm.

THE FARM LOOK

Wherever you lay out the market, keep thinking that the people are looking for an easy road for getting to you, and for signs directing them tastefully yet unconfusingly toward you. The market should strike them with a direct impression of what you have to sell and the quality of it, and it ought to have a quiet, uncrowded, inviting look about it. Get all these first glimpses right and only your competitors will be able to keep the crowds away from you. One powerful notion that surrounding farmland can give is this: The food you sell is growing right there—how can it be anything but strictly fresh? Farmhands tending the crops will be noticed too, and so will you and your helpers as you work around the market. You're not just playing the part of salesman but being all the things people expect a retailing farmer to be—friendly, easygoing, busy but interested in helping, and full of knowledge about really good produce. But dirt and lounging about are not part of the picture they look forward to, especially those of the so-called gentler sex.

RED TAPE

It's as true as ever that you can't even say boo to your wife without getting an okay from some bureaucrat (or is it the other way around?). Starting in business takes a square yard or so of confusing paperwork. Your county agricultural agent can warn you on most of the rules to be aware of and how to do what the rules say you must and must not do. A license to operate a retail foodselling business is just the beginning, though a costly one. Find out well in advance of starting up how many of the rules listed here you'll have to do something about, which of them apply to a market of the size and type you're planning, how much these pieces of paper will cost you (it could add a large chunk to the first-year expenses), and if you'll have to meet still more requirements.

Here I've collected some of these rules:

(1) *grading laws* that regulate the size and quality you must build into the foods you sell.

(2) *zoning laws* saying what you can build where (if they allow you to build at all) and how much space you must allow for parking lot, entrances to it, and exits.

(3) *environmental laws* telling you *if* you can build and how, and what you'll have to do with any wastes you may generate.

(4) *health regulations* to be sure your produce and market don't give the customers something more than they bargained for, like the plague.

(5) *consumer protection laws* so that people will be sure they get all they pay for and nothing will be misrepresented.

(6) *sales tax laws* to pay for all the regulating and inspecting the state does to keep you in line.

(7) *labeling laws* to make the public sure you're giving them the good things you seem to be offering for sale.

(8) *weights and measures laws* to assure everyone of getting a fair shake for his money.

(9) *blue laws* that tell you when you can sell what.

(10) *building permits and inspections* to make your structures safe for the public and yourself.

(11) *highway setback rules* to keep you back from the road, which you don't want to be too close to anyway.

(12) *wages and hours laws* to keep you from abusing your rights as an employer, if you should happen to be one.

(13) *parking regulations* to reassure the customers that they can safely visit you and look at your goods without damage to themselves and their property.

(14) *laws governing signs* (see Chapter 7) and other advertising, so that you won't mess up the countryside with strident messages about the wonderful things you offer for sale.

(15) *fire and police regulations* that anyone would be silly to ignore.

Rising above all the rules is the law of good conscience, compelling you to obey all these limiting and directing regulations for the good of everyone. The red tape may look like one big nuisance, but the rules are there to make us all reasonably sure that everyone else is doing business decently. Without them the unscrupulous would multiply and be even more common than they are now.

Better get to know the people who run the departments of trade, commerce and taxation of your town, county and state. Qualifying for and living up to their licenses can be the most difficult and expensive parts of getting started. The costs will have to be figured into your operating expenses.

CREATE THE MARKET

Now's the time to leap into the part of the planning job that may stretch your imagination and might even be fun, though it means you may soon be spending lots of money. If you've never gotten into any planning as ambitious as this, don't let the size of it disturb you—plenty of help is available for this part of your project, much of it without cost. All you have to know is whom to ask and where to find them. I have a few suggestions; the rest can be had from your county extension and agriculture department experts.

How big can it be? Decide first how big a market you can handle. The size is best settled by the audience or market you will be selling to. You don't really need sophisticated marketing research to find that out, though it won't hurt to do some careful sniffing around. The size of the marketplace sets the volume or amount of product you will sell and the number of dollars you will take in. Starting at the bottom, finding the lower limits on how much business you will do, is fairly easy to estimate. You may want to be just a dabbler in this retailing business, either permanently or just for a start. And that's fine for someone who intends to sell only surplus from a big hobby garden or the excess off the top of produce sold to wholesalers or retailers. It's a way to get a little extra money.

You are reading this book though, and that means to me that you expect to make a real business—small or middle-sized—of your market. For that you need the land, at least a few hardworking acres producing harvests, and a small building with say one or two thousand square feet of space. Anyone who tried to make money with less of a physical start than that might do all right but would be shrinking his chances a little. Restricting the investment can cut down on the profits; it doesn't always reduce the difficulties. The benefits of scale show up in most businesses. Up to a limit, bigger investments bring bigger profits. Do what you can to avoid wasting your resources on a too-small business. Leave to the kids the roadside table with a couple of boxes of backyard-grown vegetables or fruits that may be good only for pocket money.

One necessity for the market shows up immediately: Most markets need sweet corn to get along. M. C. Goldman, in *Organic Gardening and Farming,* October, 1972, tells how a woman in Massachusetts who has just a few acres makes a point of earning $2,000 an acre on corn and other produce. Another farmer in Massachusetts earned $11,000 in produce in a season, $3,000 of it on corn. He had only eight acres of corn, but planted every nine days from late April to late July. Another earned $10,000 from only 25 acres a few years ago. The secret seems to be not lots of acres but frequent harvests on a few acres. That gives you enough volume to keep the customers coming back all through the season. Read more about corn specializing in Chapter 9.

Add it up. If you've been a grower, add up the production figures, the amount you think you can draw out of your land and feed into your market. Then look into the services you think you can give to customers. Decide which crops you will sell. That will help settle the kind and size of market you should end up with. See your banker to talk of limits on the amount you can plow into it. Then talk with an architect or find some blueprints and get estimates on materials. To do the construction work yourself you'll need detailed plans. If you won't be your own designer, get a qualified architect to suggest the type and size of structure your money will buy. Ask around about an architect—don't just pull a name out of the yellow pages, any more than you would choose a doctor in that way. The building contractor's ability and dependability also demand close investigation if you have to have the work done. Ask a competitor with an attractive, efficient-looking structure who built it.

Building it yourself. In these days of extraordinarily high building costs you'd do well to try to find volunteers and build it yourself, especially if the helpers have some building experience. It's nice to have an adequate building, but is it worth going deep into debt? Remember that an inaccurate estimate, an inexperienced builder, or someone cutting costs in the wrong places can involve you in worthless materials, costly delays, and a lot of other complications that you can do very well without. You want people who don't have to be supervised every minute they're working. Good ones are hard to come by, but there are some out there. Much looking and luck will bring you to them. Whoever does the job, be sure to consider the inexpensive blueprints and instructions your extension agent can lead you to, and the ones shown here. Be sure, though, that the plans and your needs match closely.

Is your market not far off the road? Save signs by calling out your message visibly on the sides.

What sort of building? One large detail needn't cause you too many hours of agonized studying—the *kind* of building to plan. M. E. Cravens and others tell us that it's not one of the things that can make you a success or failure, if attracting the public is a problem. It doesn't seem to matter what kind of shelter you plan for the market—you can convert an old barn or packing house or fruit storage building, or build a shed of poles. Any old enclosure (or any new one for that matter) that keeps most of the weather out and lets the customers in freely will serve you just as well as a spanking new, expensive structure. Of course the most efficient building is the one you design to suit exactly the kind of marketing you intend to do. If you can afford that right away and know enough about the business to tell just what's needed, so much the better. Few people are in that good shape before they start out. Most will be better off starting on a small scale and waiting till experience equips them with knowledge and figures, plus money.

Let the people in. An important but not too obvious way of making sure the market's design will work for you, and not for the competition, is brought out by Lou Albano, consultant on roadside marketing for the Massachusetts Department of Agriculture. He suggests that your design be aimed specifically at making the customers part of the market—bring them right in with you instead of holding them at arm's length across a counter. Building around customers as well as the market brings both together, making the chances much bigger that the visitors will buy and probably buy more than they would as total outsiders. That probably means a good-sized structure.

Have a layout that works. Divide your market's interior and exterior into separate areas to fit the different uses: outdoor and inside displays, selling area and preparation area, aisle space and display space, prime spots for fast-moving items, and slower spots for produce that people don't go looking for but should buy anyway. Will you enclose the market on all sides all the time or have garage doors or sliding partitions to open up the front and the sides or all three?

Work space. How much work space will you need for servicing the displays and the produce? Should your ratio be two parts selling room to one part preparation room—or even higher? Will some of the getting ready be done in another building? How much space should you allow for refrigerated storage, all the time and during times when the market is shut down, as at night? How much space will fixed equipment take, and how about movable displays and stocking carts? How much room will the checkout take and where should it be? Will anything else occupy space—benches for customers or their spouses or children to rest on while the buying is going on; a "bar" for selling cider or other cold drinks—or hot drinks if your season runs long?

Plan on much window space for light and visibility from

outside. You can even surround yourself with window walls if you want to pay for them, but make sure that wherever the windows are, plenty of room is left over for display shelves, racks, and counters. The produce needs to be spread around, to be easy to see, if people are to buy several things instead of one or two. Aisles, if you plan to have any, ought to be roomy enough to hold two people abreast to let folks move around the displays easily, without jostling each other or the merchandise. Six feet should be enough to keep them apart. Read more about these displays and space in Chapter 8.

The checkout can be near the front of the store for convenience. It must be where people won't pile up around it, blocking shoppers from the displays nearby. It also can be cannily placed so that they will wander by all or most of the displays to get to the cash register, even if they came in to buy just one thing. And the aisles have to be big enough to let you move stock around with whatever equipment you use to haul produce in.

The preparation room or service area doesn't have to be stuck right out in the middle of the selling part of the market. On the other hand, that preparation room usually can't be pushed out of the market building, because produce coming in from the field must move quickly through the food dresser's hands and out into the displays.

Equipment. What other equipment will be indispensable? A sink is a necessity for getting freshly picked vegetables ready for showing. A double sink with durable finish and wide basins is what you want; equip it with a spray nozzle for washing dirt off, a drain basket, a feed-in counter for sorting and trimming, a drainboard with a lot of space for packaging (if you do any) and a cart for arranging the display. You might want to set up a conveyor system that will feed crates or bushel baskets from field to scrubber. A sturdy table next to the drainboard will give room for boxing or arranging the produce for the displays.

The *dump table,* with its unpretty name, can be extremely helpful for inspecting and grading produce. The Rhode Island Agricultural Extension Service (Kingston, R.I.) Circular 130 has plans for a simply designed dump table. It has few parts, looks easy to put together and can be used in no fewer than six ways: flat dump table, angled table with enclosed sides or without them, and with or without an elevated shelf. Keeping this preparation place separate from the selling room, even with a partial partition, is better than having everything out in the open. A door shutting it off is helpful if it is big enough to take your stocking equipment, carts, or displays from preparation to selling rooms. Whoever is working in there doesn't want to be distracted from the important task of readying goods for sale by people eager to be waited on. And it's best not to distract the public from the business they're about, which is concentrating on the finished product and on making their minds up to buy.

Keep people moving. If you plan a big enough market, you'll be interested in customer flow. Ransom A. Blakeley, formerly assistant professor and Marketing Specialist at Purdue University, analyzed how customers moved around typical markets and proved that planning the routes they are most likely to take will make it easier for you to be sure they're exposed to everything you have to sell. We show his planning sequence in Figure 3.1 to give you an idea of how important it can be to spread things around thoughtfully, with attention-getting displays scattered among the items people don't always go for directly. Of course, if your market is the size of a telephone booth and you don't want it to grow, not much that we say in this section will be of use to you.

Also in the back room is the *refrigerated storage area,* which is a hard thing to do without in the heat of summer. How big should that be? Roomy enough to hold anything that can't sit around unprotected against destructive heat overnight, and to store delicate replenishments for displays all the time. The cold room also needs a wide door; it can do without windows.

Among other pieces of equipment you probably will need are *skids* or *wheeled tables* for storing and moving around large amounts of produce; *scales* for packaging and pricing; *more scales* for customers to weigh their own purchases on; *trash cans* with covers; *crate hammers* for getting at shipped-in produce; *apple polishers; pea and bean shellers;* an *adding machine* and a *cash register* (or both in one).

Fig. 3.1. Analyzing movement of customers for an efficiently designed market.

Step 1: Flow sheets for individual customers (100).

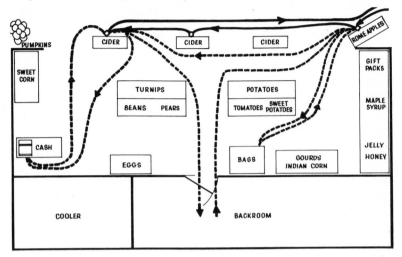

Key: --- Clerk flow —— Customer flow

Step 2: All individual flow charts combined on selling area layout (customer version; similar chart needed on clerk flow).

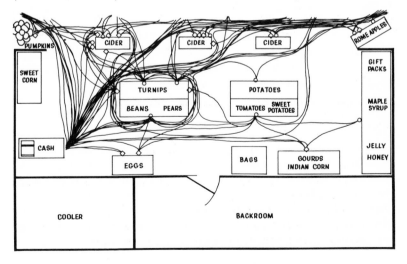

Step 3 (A): Problems identified from step 2.

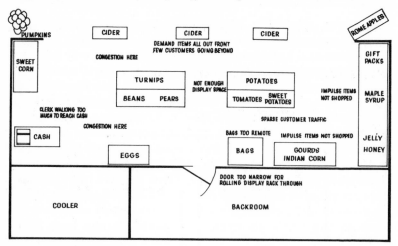

Step 3 (B): Improved layout.

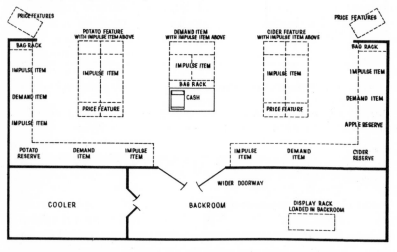

Improvements

1. Demand items spaced to induce people to examine the whole market; always with impulse items adjacent.
2. More variety in the front.
3. Eliminate small cider tables that obstructed foot traffic flow into market.
4. Display space nearly doubled.
5. Bags and cash more conveniently located. Cash in center to cut down walking and reduce corner congestion.

Lighting. Planning to keep the market open for an extended season or at night for extra income? Talk to the local power and light company. If you like, they will have a lighting engineer do a survey of the lights you will need and their cost, usually without charge. Plan to mix fluorescent and incandescent lights, for both brightness and good color. But keep the lighting within reason. Overdoing it will give the glaring supermarket look and add unnecessary, *big* cost. White fluorescent lights change the colors of your fruits and vegetables. Red things look muddy; yellow vegetables and fruits look greenish and unripe. The "cool white" bulbs simply don't give off light at the red end of the spectrum. The simple solution? Replace these bulbs with lamps which come closer to the sun's spectrum and make things look like themselves.

A few spot and flood lamps will draw eyes to featured displays to encourage impulse buying. Outdoor lights to dramatize the market and illuminate the parking area for safety and easy moving about may be necessary, too. Buglights around the outside may keep some nuisance visitors away. And if you have interesting-looking rocks, bushes, or trees around the market, a small spotlight can make them part of your natural appeal.

PARKING MATTERS

Think out your accommodations for the people driving into your welcoming lot, parking there and getting out again. As long as you're asking them to drop by, make it easy for them. This is one service to the public that's noticed whether it's handled properly *or* inadequately. Ease, safety, convenience are your goals. Some people starting out have been known to think they can just let the parking area happen.

As they see it, if the market has a few feet of open dirt on one side or another that's all the parking area the customer needs. But a bit of planning will pay off. Estimate how many cars might land on your grounds at your peak times—say on

a beautiful summer weekend when everything's ripening at once. You might one day look up and see yourself surrounded by parked and parking cars.

Space for cars. To fit these oversized groups in you'll need, first, plenty of space. In this space plan a separate wide entrance and exit that will funnel even timid drivers out and into traffic gently, not abruptly. Each way in or out must be marked with a clear sign, visible day or night, if people are to use the area as you wish. With luck or careful planning you have enough frontage on the road to be sure that cars, entering and departing, from both directions at once, won't get in their own way. If it's hard or dangerous to get into or out of your lot you'll scare customers away almost as fast as high prices would.

How big a lot? Look around at markets with parking areas of about the size you expect yours to be and arrive at an average size, then add 25 to 50 per cent to it for good measure. The county or municipal highway department is a good place to start learning how to plan. From them you may get specifications on minimum size, proper placement, and any required markings. The zoning or planning board and conservation commission can give guidance, too. A most important thing to know is that the parking area's surface probably shouldn't be plain dirt. People don't want to get their sneakers or shiny cars dusty or muddy. A market with some size to it will take extra work cleaning the parking lot off the floor many times a day. A dirt lot with poor drainage soon will be a rutted mess. Gravel dressing seems the most often used for smaller markets. It doesn't cost a lot, is easy to spread, and looks fine if it's touched up often. Of course it isn't very durable when the weather stays bad and traffic is heavy. Only asphalt will take that kind of beating. But many people think the neat, lasting, easy-to-mark hard surface gives the market too much of a commercial look. The initial cost of permanent coating is quite high, too. A season or two ought to tell you if the investment is justifiable.

Expect expansion. One rule for knowing how much space you'll need says to allow fifteen spaces for every hundred cars you expect to see coming in each day. On the other hand, if you're going to have a big business from the start, double the space, allowing for future expansion right away, put a hard surface on it, and mark it clearly with lanes and spaces. Right-angle parking is probably the most useful way to lay out such a lot. It gives most capacity, allows for easy two-way movement, demands few barriers, and cuts the distance drivers have to move around as they get into and out of the lot. A package pickup lane may save weak backs if it, too, is well marked.

The parking area has to be worked into your market plan carefully to hold off common nuisances. Putting all that space out front of the market means people will see not the market but cars, obscuring displays or the whole place. One or both sides of the building may be the best place to put parking areas, but a market surrounded by cars is neither pleasant nor visible. Set aside a free view to the fields for the customers who may want to see where you work your magic. Above all, make it clear with signs or barriers just where people ought to come and go, and give them lots of room for error so that they won't hurt each other out of confusion or tight spacing.

WHEN DO YOU DO THE MARKETING?

If you've set your mind on going into the roadside business, you must know the time market operation can take out of your days. As a producer you may have an idea of how long the hours can be. But this business has a difference. It's not just getting through one job at a time—feeling the satisfaction when all crops are in the ground, or delivering a harvest into the market, or sowing, tilling, fertilizing, weeding. Instead it's a matter of putting most of your waking hours into tending the store, every day in the season. You may not be busy every minute, but you do have to be right there for many hours every day. May as well make out a schedule telling where and at which hours you and everyone else working in the market will be for the next year. Someone has to be around with bright eyes and pleasant manner when the customers show up, and if you're making it a family endeavor that can mean a ten- or twelve-hour day for some or all of you.

Working hours. Figure how many hours in a day you can profitably keep the market open, then how many in the week, month, and season. Fit into this equation the many factors that will help you know how to keep the business moving: the amount of produce that will be coming in each day, the number of customers you can expect hour by hour, how much time you can spare from other duties (such as growing the produce), willingness and ability of the family to help, and availability of extra help from outside. These, plus health and ambition, will be your limits. Here, too, your competitors can be useful as you estimate your hours and seasons. Your schedule may be altogether different, but it's reassuring to know how much time other people put in.

If you prefer a short season so that you can diddle around for the rest of the year spending the money you've earned, then the number of hours you stay open each day and the length of your selling season will be as long as you can make them. In fact, you'll probably have to cram in all the time you can just to make a profit in some years. Eight or nine o'clock in the morning to eight or nine at night may be your standard work day, and you'd better plan to keep the market open every day of the week. Any time a customer comes by and the shop is shut down your profits shrink. The standard season in many parts of the country is April to October, stretchable, of course, by handling things other than fresh produce or by growing crops under glass.

Advertising your hours. Let the customers know, by advertisement or signs, when you're there to do business and when your season starts and ends. Include your daily hours and a phone number where they can call to find out if they've forgotten. It's hard to forgive the marketer who isn't around to sell you food you need, after you've driven an hour to get there. To parcel out your time you can figure that your peak selling days will be Saturday and Sunday, morning or afternoon or both. It's just that more people get out to shop on weekends, even if most of your trade is local. And they seem more relaxed about their shopping on a weekend, possibly even freer with their money. The rest of the week goes from an early slump to a steadily rising curve. Some marketers make 40 percent of their sales in the first four days of the week, then ring up 60 percent on Friday, Saturday and Sunday.

Who are the customers? Quite a few of your buying, selling, and growing practices may depend on the type of people you'll be dealing with most. Do a little preliminary market research. Big marketers won't do a thing until they have all the knowledge they can gather or buy about how many people might be in the market for their goods, what customers are most likely to want, when they'll expect to find the food for sale, and where to put their selling efforts to reach the biggest number of people. Are these people affluent? Are they close neighbors of yours? Do they shop around for the best produce, or the cheapest, or only the staples, or something special like berries? How often do they shop? Twice a week or once in a while? How do they decide where to shop for produce? What do they buy? Are Sunday

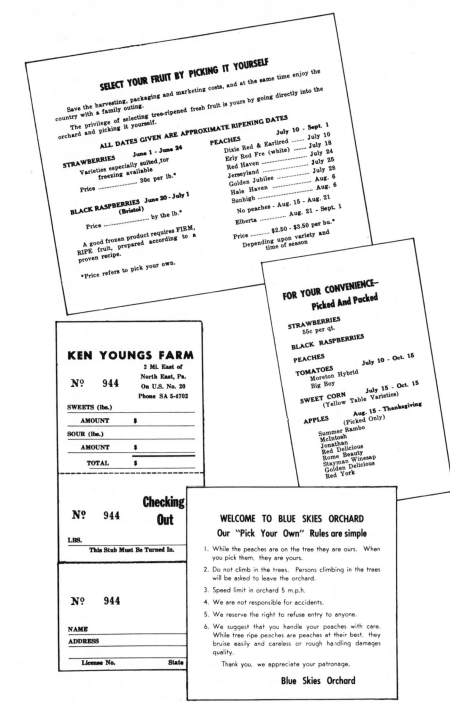

SELECT YOUR FRUIT BY PICKING IT YOURSELF

Save the harvesting, packaging and marketing costs, and at the same time enjoy the country with a family outing.

The privilege of selecting tree-ripened fresh fruit is yours by going directly into the orchard and picking it yourself.

ALL DATES GIVEN ARE APPROXIMATE RIPENING DATES

STRAWBERRIES   June 1 - June 24

Varieties especially suited for freezing available

Price .... 30c per lb.*

BLACK RASPBERRIES June 20 - July 1
(Bristol)

Price .... by the lb.*

A good frozen product requires FIRM, RIPE fruit, prepared according to a proven recipe.

*Price refers to pick your own.

PEACHES   July 10 - Sept. 1

Dixie Red & Earlired .... July 10
Erly Red Fre (white) .... July 18
Red Haven .... July 24
Jerseyland .... July 25
Golden Jubilee .... July 28
Hale Haven .... Aug. 6
Sunhigh .... Aug. 6

No peaches - Aug. 15 - Aug. 21

Elberta .... Aug. 21 - Sept. 1

Price .... $2.50 - $3.50 per bu.*
Depending upon variety and
time of season

FOR YOUR CONVENIENCE—
Picked And Packed

STRAWBERRIES
55c per qt.

BLACK RASPBERRIES

PEACHES   July 10 - Oct. 15

TOMATOES
Moreton Hybrid
Big Boy

SWEET CORN   July 15 - Oct. 15
(Yellow Table Varieties)

APPLES   Aug. 15 - Thanksgiving
(Picked Only)

Summer Rambo
McIntosh
Jonathan
Red Delicious
Rome Beauty
Stayman Winesap
Golden Delicious
Red York

KEN YOUNGS FARM

2 Mi. East of
North East, Pa.
On U.S. No. 20
Phone SA 5-4702

Nº 944

SWEETS (lbs.) _____

AMOUNT $ _____

SOUR (lbs.) _____

AMOUNT $ _____

TOTAL $ _____

- - - - - - - - - - - - - - - - - - -

Nº 944   **Checking
Out**

LBS.

This Stub Must Be Turned In.

Nº 944

NAME

ADDRESS

License No.   State

WELCOME TO BLUE SKIES ORCHARD
Our "Pick Your Own" Rules are simple

1. While the peaches are on the tree they are ours. When you pick them, they are yours.

2. Do not climb in the trees. Persons climbing in the trees will be asked to leave the orchard.

3. Speed limit in orchard 5 m.p.h.

4. We are not responsible for accidents.

5. We reserve the right to refuse entry to anyone.

6. We suggest that you handle your peaches with care. While tree ripe peaches are peaches at their best, they bruise easily and careless or rough handling damages quality.

Thank you, we appreciate your patronage,

Blue Skies Orchard

drivers or local neighbors most likely to make up your audience? Are they young families mostly or oldsters?

The most recent news that I've seen on who the customers are comes from a study done by the Life Sciences and Agriculture Experiment Station of the University of Maine. The Maine study confirms most ideas I've reported here, with differences because of that region's peculiarities (not, of course, that Maine is any more peculiar than any other place). In the stands they surveyed, which were open ten hours a day, at least several days a week, from late June till late October (200 days altogether), 86 percent of the customers were regulars. They were year-round residents of the area, making a special trip to buy one or more of the 36 vegetables, fruits or non-produce items sold at these stands. Most were in middle- to higher-income brackets and came to buy one or two items specifically. Two-thirds of them spent less than two dollars on their favorite items—corn, tomatoes, cucumbers, lettuce, squash, beans, potatoes and carrots. The stands served about ten customers an hour. The biggest purchases were made by people with large families. Most often the woman of the family was doing the shopping, and she drove 7.5 miles to get to the market. The people who had farthest to drive, as we'd expect, bought more than nearby residents or families just out for a ride. A fact that the researchers turned up was that people shopping at a market for the first time usually were younger and less well off than the regular customers, though all bought about the same amount. Once again, here's that clear hint: Most of your advertising and selling attention are best poured onto your dependable regulars, not the untried masses who may be out there somewhere.

HOW DO YOU DO THE MARKETING?

The large numbers of people coming and going in and around the market make it very clear that anyone who works there had best be mentally equipped to exert himself for every customer, not just concentrating on those who at once seem friendly and eager to buy. You've got to size up customers in an instant, whether they know the market or are newcomers. The people will be very different, but as you meet and watch them and get used to dealing with all kinds, you may be surprised to find how they sort themselves into recognizable types of personalities and faces.

Trying to predict how they will behave, of course, is like straining to guess the next snowflake's shape. The regulars know pretty much what they want, and probably they have made a special effort to come out and get it. The itinerant or transient people who, depending on where you are, may be vacationers, tourists just passing through, holiday travelers visiting family or friends, weekend joyriders—all these are best reached by your market's appealing looks and displays in which quality is evident. They are the ones most likely to succumb to the marketer's ally, impulse buying—on which all retailers depend for a good part of their sales. These droppers-in may have no thought of buying anything when they arrive, yet if their minds are open you have a chance to sell something to them. For those who come from not far away, the first visit is a chance for you to make repeat customers of them, which is your most important goal.

To the customer who has no clear idea of what to buy, you can add the one attracted by word-of-mouth recommendation from previously pleased customers, or by advertising of any kind that reaches its mark. Your customers will be receptive to some of your market's benefits, untouched by others. It wouldn't do to leave any of them unreached by the good service you can give them. Treat all warmly and informatively, and see how big a percentage of them you can turn into paying customers. People do spend billions a year on food. You stand a perfectly good chance of getting some of that money, *but* it takes thought and work.

Chapter 4

The Working Market and

How to Manage It

Once the market is running freely, with all your first doubts and delays cleared away, you might find time for a sobering look back at the battles you've won or lost. But take a suggestion—make that reassessment early, before you open for a new season if possible. Even if you've been a working producer, the thought may come to mind "How do I know all about running a retail business if I've never done it before?" Save later trouble and realize now that waiting to learn by doing is not the best way to start a business, nor is it likely to swamp you with quick riches.

First, pick out every useful-looking idea that turns up in this book (it's the only one in print for the moment). Think long about each idea; then *do* something about one of them. Try one to get the project in motion. Whether or not the first one works, get yourself set to try another. Then go on through your list of what has to be done now, and what can really wait till later. Progress may be slow in coming, but the simple action of, say, calling on the agricultural extension agent with a handful of questions will help get your starting problems out where you can see them.

Second, talk to neighboring marketers and farmers. Ask about their problems. Almost anyone will share a problem, and some may tell their solutions. Learning by others' trials and errors is pretty painless; people are proud to talk of difficulties when they're solved.

Third, spread some of your fired-up planning energy among the details sown in this chapter. Maybe you think common sense will handle these small matters. It will, but only when you know they're there.

THE MANAGER AT WORK

Let's go over the most important parts of the business you'll have to manage, like managing the physical market. Most markets, of course, don't manage themselves, though the most efficient of them give that impression. Whether it's a little one-room affair or a sizable building, whether you are the whole staff, or your family helps out, or you have a dozen people working full time, everything has to be fitted together to work smoothly, and that means managing. If you'd rather not keep a hundred things in mind at the same time, do some of the managerial work by the checklist method. Before the season starts, make up a takeoff checklist covering the market outside and inside, and everything that has to be ready to go by opening day. Then start up a weekly checklist to remind yourself of the daily in-season things that need tending to. If you get these tickler lists working well in the early, perhaps slow-moving days, then the later, possibly rushed times won't catch you unprepared.

Clean up. An easy and yet vital item to cover in the list is something that might not be noticed if nothing is wrong but certainly will hit anyone in the face if it's *not* tended to—cleanliness and neatness of your people, produce and physical facilities. Rusty and disintegrating bits of equipment and material outside the market that lie where they fell are a good place to start. An informal atmosphere doesn't mean a junky-looking one. An old wagon or sleigh or other piece of antique equipment that is kept up carefully gives an air of country authenticity; an old hulk of

machinery or a decaying old car gives a very different impression. A pile of manure may be an impressive organic touch, but it will turn more people away than anything else but rotten food. A good housekeeper will make the cleanliness noticeable to people who want to know they're getting the cleanest food anywhere. The visitor should be able to eat your produce off the surfaces in your market. Keep windows sparkling, too, because they show dirt first. Anyone dealing directly with the public must be impressively neat about everything. Usually dressing decently in clean, attractive and not too unconventional clothes impresses most people favorably. Clean jeans and bright shirts are okay, but shirtless overalls are less pleasant. Think about hair on face and head as restaurant people have to—if it's neat, it will offend no one.

Cleaning doesn't have to be a miserable task if you're prepared to do it on a schedule and have the tools it takes. Many very helpful ideas can be found in Ransom A. Blakeley's *Tips for Easier Cleaning,* available from Purdue University (see bibliography). Here are a few of them.

Do it regularly. Regular cleanups make life easier by holding back the buildup of dirt that means harder work and more time spent scrubbing. They also keep the market free of decay, smells, and visible dirtiness. You might decide on a one-week schedule for cleaning all display fixtures, daily or at least weekly mopping for the floors and cleaning for the windows, and once-a-month attacks on lighting fixtures, walls and woodwork. But do put together a schedule.

Plan for cleanliness. Like anything else, you can simplify cleanups by planning. When you build or remodel, pick building materials with smooth, nonporous, non-absorbent surfaces. Plastic cove molding for baseboards protects walls and saves painting and also keeps dirt from gathering. If your display equipment is wheeled, it will be easy to clean everywhere on the floors. It also can be designed with space underneath for the one who is cleaning to get at floor dirt. Anything that's hard to reach under will accumulate plenty of debris.

Cheap cleaning equipment is of less than no use. Invest in professional tools and cleaning solutions. Mops, buckets, wringers, and vacuum cleaners ought to be the best. Good equipment and easy-to-get-at storage space encourages helpers to regular efforts, speedy work, and rapid attention to spills. Work out an arrangement that will keep the equipment organized for quick accessibility, and have a hot water outlet nearby.

SMELLS

Cleaning should be done as a professional would tackle it, like all the other special jobs you must do or oversee in a market. This kind of cleaning will cure many ailments (even flabby muscles). Bugs don't bother a spotless market. And dirty appearance can't last long under attack by strong cleansers. But another uncleanness is harder to destroy because it has the underhanded advantage of being subtle, and that is *smells.* Ransom Blakeley's *Essence of Your Market: Making Dollars from Scents,* gives still more guidance, and most of the ideas that follow come from that publication.

The market should be a clean, fresh background against which all its foods and flowers can display their true aromas. One piece of over-ripe fruit or a spot on the floor that the mop missed can make a carefully run market smell a little like a garbage dump.

Hire a smell spotter. Of course you adapt yourself to the smells in your own market quickly and thoroughly, so that you can't be relied on to tell if something's rotten in a corner; you're adapted to the market's good smells and its bad ones. And most customers are too polite to say you're harboring putrefaction somewhere. Solve the adaptation problem by having a neighbor (a non-smoker between 15 and 45 years old, because that's the age span for best smellers) come in and do some olfactory detective work. Might be a good idea to do that once a week.

Cleansing breezes. Ventilation is good first aid for a stale-smelling room, because it leads winds past the source of an odor so quickly that odor molecules in the air can't build up enough for a nose to notice.

Cigarette, cigar, and pipe smoke have a way of clinging to and penetrating paper products such as bags and cardboard boxes, and persisting for months. A NO SMOKING sign and strict enforcement of that policy will cure this condition, keep your foods from being contaminated by the nicotine smell, and please your many non-smoking customers, too.

Removing smells. Chemical preparations can mask or neutralize some odors, but their effect is very specific. Cleaners and some insecticides that have ammonia or pine oil may combine with the ethylene gas given off by ripening fruits and flowers. Together, they can make an obnoxious odor. Cleaners containing formalin (formaldehyde) in effect deodorize the customer's nose if not the market, but they remove all pleasant odors along with the nasty ones.

Polyethlene bags will let some food odors in and out, but polypropylene film keeps odors in and around the product.

Polyvinyl chloride (PVC) bags are now suspected of causing cancer. They are no longer wrapped around luncheon meats, at least, the papers announced in 1975.

Watch out for lawn fertilizers that contain weed killers, such as 2-4D. Their smell is irritating and they can kill broadleaf plants displayed in the building. Keep those fertilizers in a separate building.

Deodorize your market by first removing from it all odor-producing substances. Soap, hot water, and elbow grease are the best solution for eliminating the odors left behind. An odorless soap and a stiff-bristled brush will get rid of decaying organic matter.

Restrooms need frequent and thorough cleaning. Activated charcoal can help, a little of this and baking soda in the wash water will neutralize restroom acids, stopping bacterial action that makes toilets smell.

When you put both flowers and vegetables in cold storage, separate them, and remember that butter, eggs, and cheeses can take up odors from cabbages and onions.

REPAIRS AND IMPROVEMENTS

Markets that are rickety and in tatters inspire no confidence. No, you don't have to keep everything covered with layers of white paint outside and in—though that won't hurt. But watch siding, roof, and paint job for signs of wear, and get at them before they grow worse. Keep doors, windows, and other movable things fixed so that they will move without forcing. There's more about maintenance needs in Chapter 8. Spiffing up the market before the season starts or before a grand opening doesn't mean dressing it in promotional plastic finery like a new chain store. But I guarantee that setting up a neat, uncluttered, working-order market won't lose you any customers.

They're tax-deductible. As you go over everything in opening a market, remember that the costs for maintenance can be deducted from your taxes as a business expense or as depreciation. List everything that costs as soon as you pay for it—you'll find it impossible to remember it all at tax return time. This review helps get you in the habit of keeping up with repairs, too. The progress checklist has both purposes: keeping the freshening and repairing taken care of and giving you a calendar telling when what got done. From this schedule you can look ahead and know when it will need doing again. You'll also know when money will have to be spent on repairs. That, too, can be useful in tax planning.

Look outside, too. Going back outside the market for a minute, you realize that landscaping is not going to take care of itself. Even if it's as simple a matter as getting decorative plantings in on time, your checklist ought to keep you up with the regular necessities, like being sure the surroundings stay green and flowering throughout the season. Prettiness attracts, and it also convinces people that you tend to business and quality. A market that is good-looking inside and out and all around suggests that the produce you sell there is likely to be just as carefully tended.

While you check over the things that need doing before you open for the season or for the first time, keep thinking about improvements that could be made by rearranging, adding, or subtracting things. Constant review from the very beginning doesn't mean reshuffling for the sake of change; but putting together a lot of little changes may make a big difference in the market's efficiency. You need a system that makes you stop and think regularly, questioning everything that's going on. That way, you'll be open to changes that might never be noticed if you didn't frequently stand back to look at the whole picture.

EVALUATE YOUR MARKET AS CUSTOMERS SEE IT

Compared with the competition, my market is:

Appearance	Poor	Behind	Same	Better	Superb
1. Are displays full and inviting?	____	____	____	____	____
2. Are color contrasts good?	____	____	____	____	____
3. Have you set out an interesting variety?	____	____	____	____	____
4. Is lighting adequate?	____	____	____	____	____
5. Do morning shoppers have full selection?	____	____	____	____	____
6. Is the floor clean?	____	____	____	____	____
7. Are displays clean?	____	____	____	____	____
8. Is parking lot free of trash?	____	____	____	____	____
9. Is all refuse out of displays?	____	____	____	____	____
10. Is produce clean for handling?	____	____	____	____	____

Convenience

	Poor	Behind	Same	Better	Superb
1. Do customers have enough room to move among display fixtures?	____	____	____	____	____

2. Can everything be
reached easily? _____ _____ _____ _____ _____

3. Is the cash register
centrally located? _____ _____ _____ _____ _____

4. Is parking safe
and easy? _____ _____ _____ _____ _____

5. Has produce been
utilized where
possible? _____ _____ _____ _____ _____

Merchandising

1. Is the feature display
magnetic? _____ _____ _____ _____ _____

2. Are all products
identified? _____ _____ _____ _____ _____

3. Do display signs
suggest serving
ideas? _____ _____ _____ _____ _____

4. Have you set up
taste-testing and cut
fruit? _____ _____ _____ _____ _____

5. Are recipes displayed
with uncommon
items? _____ _____ _____ _____ _____

Personnel

1. Do they seem to
enjoy their work? _____ _____ _____ _____ _____

2. Is a special service
rendered promptly? _____ _____ _____ _____ _____

3. Are clerks efficient
   and not in the
   customer's way?   ____ ____ ____ ____ ____

4. Is personal service
   courteous and
   cheerful?   ____ ____ ____ ____ ____

5. Are clerks well
   groomed and neat?
   Aprons clean?   ____ ____ ____ ____ ____

Quality

1. Are top grades
   featured?   ____ ____ ____ ____ ____

2. Are temperatures
   low enough for highly
   perishable reserve
   stocks?   ____ ____ ____ ____ ____

3. Are culls removed for
   discount pricing?   ____ ____ ____ ____ ____

4. Are green vegetables
   moist and sparkling? ____ ____ ____ ____ ____

5. Has ripe fruit been
   marked down?   ____ ____ ____ ____ ____

Value

1. Are prices clearly
   marked?   ____ ____ ____ ____ ____

2. Are prices fair and
   competitive?   ____ ____ ____ ____ ____

3. Are sale units
   posted?   ____ ____ ____ ____ ____

4. Are high-value
   seasonal items
   featured?   ____   ____   ____   ____   ____

5. Are sizes (as for
   pumpkins) separated
   for pricing?   ____   ____   ____   ____   ____

WATCH THE DETAILS

Why all this fuss about details? When people come to the country looking for produce they expect country atmosphere, don't they? Well, even the ones from nearby who visit the market often and become friends aren't going to overlook the little unpleasant things. And this is one place where you can beat the competition only by joining it. Big supermarkets are kept impressively clean at all times, at least on the surface. People are used to that expensively policed cleanliness. If you can give them that as well as top-quality food and homely, friendly, efficient service, they'll feel at ease. The little mistakes or missed spots have to be noticed by you, first. Borrow the customer's eyes and nose as a practiced manager must.

Be a friend. Watch yourself at work dealing with the public, and keep an eye on anyone working with you. The impersonal, chilly aloofness that many people put on because they feel customers expect it is *not* pleasant. Everyone handling your customers ought to have a warm, welcoming attitude, even under fire from an irate customer who's been rubbed the wrong way about something real or imaginary. It can be a great feeling to turn an angry complainer into a satisfied friend of the market. It's a trying experience but worth a consistent effort to be friendly.

People need psychological reasons for coming back to your market as well as the direct, practical things like foods of superb taste, plenty of conveniences, and pleasing appearance. You want people to feel that your market is sensibly arranged to avoid confusing them; uncrowded, which gives the same effect; and so wholesome that they just don't have to worry about shopping at your place or eating the food you sell. Physical comforts help too. Shade trees and awnings for summer heat, heating for chilly spring and fall days, benches or chairs inside and out for resting before or after shopping, maybe even a picnic place for summer days and a roaring fire in fireplace or stove around the fall and winter holidays.

Sell good produce. The produce itself is the second of your managerial responsibilities. Where does it come from? That's the question I ask myself when I visit a market for the first time. Is it all home-grown, and for that reason absolutely fresh and carefully grown? Or, almost as good, does everything come from the owner's farm and other local farms that grow equally good food? Or does the marketer get it where ordinary retailers do, from the wholesale warehouse where things are shipped in from thousands of miles away, not necessarily freshly harvested and ripened on the plant? The non-producer's market may have very low prices, but I'm one of the many who takes an interest in the food I eat. I look for quality first and price second.

Your way of getting produce from the field to the display tables will have to depend on your resources, of course. If the fields are your own, the truck or tractor and wagon, with crates or baskets packed by you and your helpers are all you need. But speedy transfer is vital to hold your advantage over commercial marketers. When you stock the market with a truck, your own or a commercial trucker's, be sure that the loading and unloading are done with gentleness. Has anything been done to the goods before they were crated? One reason for buying some produce from other growers is that the farmer who specializes in growing them will sell them to you ready to display and retail, so that you have no worries about preparation and handling.

Keep inventory. How do you know what you have on hand to sell from day to day? A regular inventory system is part of any business that sells a product. Once you've got the market going, you'll need to know how much to harvest each day, or how much to buy from your other sources. With a careful inventory it's easier to end the day and the week with empty shelves, or at least with the least possible produce that has to be stored, losing quality as it ages.

Anyone not new to the business can use the day-to-day sales records from previous years to know how much may be sold, harvested, or bought on such and such a day. When starting out, be sure to keep these records accurately; the business can't flourish without them. If you store leftovers in a cooler, mark each crate or basket with an X each night. If you display everything in crates or boxes, mark each with a check if it has been carried over unsold, with another check for each day it doesn't sell. Then move it to the quick-sale, marked-down display while it's still good but about ready to show its age. Or use the letter-dating method: *A* for Monday through *F* for Saturday. Bulk displays are a little harder to follow as they get on in age. Merchandise in those sells quickest from the center, so that you can move things from edges, front and back into the middle as the display empties.

LIVING MERCHANDISE HOLDS ITS QUALITY

Wherever your products come from, you know one fact about them: that as living things they deteriorate from the moment they are picked. Speed in handling is your first order of business. Apply gentleness along with that speed to be sure that every item will be in prime selling condition—not cut, bruised, scratched, dirty, discolored or lacking parts. And use your inventory control so as not to pick or buy too much to sell in a day, especially if you have no cooling facilities. Clear from your shelves merchandise that's suffering from old age—mark it down. That also gives the thrifty customer a break. Check everything for age each night in the hottest part of the season. Constant watchfulness is one secret you'll need for success. Put up a "day old" special at the back of the market; it may give you more sales volume and keep this elderly, substandard, lower-priced merchandise from cutting into sales of your fresher stock. Make this quick-sale merchandise a real bargain for people who want to buy it for preserving, especially in large quantities; mark the price down by at least half. That will move it a lot faster than dropping it by only a quarter or less of the original price, which could defeat your purpose by leaving you with a lot of unsold produce—and no profit at all.

Keep it fresh. Losses to spoilage can devour profits, but it's better that *you* discover unexpected aging than have a customer find it dribbling odorously down her dress. Everything you offer for sale has to be fresh as life or you're in the wrong business. Fresh fruits and vegetables are breathing beings. The breathing idea surprises many people, but its consequence is serious. Breathing uses enzymes to burn oxygen, combining that with plant sugars and giving off carbon dioxide and heat. The heat fuels more of the reaction, piling up more and more deterioration. The most perishable foods simply use oxygen more rapidly and deteriorate faster—peas, berries, corn and peaches for instance.

The physiological changes that go on in corn are noticed by many because it changes so drastically inside, though it doesn't show the wear and tear as clearly on the outside—certainly not with the husk unbroken. The customer is very much at your mercy here, and will eventually show gratitude for your attentions by hurrying back for more if you can promise and provide freshness. The public shouldn't have to think about the enzymes steaming away inside that can change more than half corn's sweetness—its sugar content—into less tasty starch in just one day even at 40° Fahrenheit. Keeping it on display on hot days or in direct sunlight can quickly destroy the goodness that nature and you worked to put there. With refrigeration, and by keeping most of the corn reasonably fresh by displaying a smaller quantity, you'll save quality, customers, and profit for another day. It's comforting to know that the corn will slow its wasting enzyme action when it's refrigerated, losing only 5 per cent of its sugar in a day. It would shock people to think how many supermarket ears they've eaten that had almost no sugar left. Think of strawberries, too, respiring ten times as fast at 40 degrees as at 32. Even relatively long-lasting apples sitting around at 70 degrees lose as much life in one day as they do in ten days at 32 degrees. Only by controlling temperature and moisture loss—plus careful handling—can you be sure you're selling the quality you advertise. Read more about handling and selling corn in Chapter 8.

A few fresh bushels of corn have strong appeal.

Handle it gently. The rule that calls for careful handling applies both to customers and yourself. All the way from harvest to dinner table, only gentle care can save the appearance and the quality hidden beneath. Remember too that all fruits and vegetables, even when washed, are covered with invisible bacteria and usually invisible mold spores. Some of these microbes are harmless, yet when conditions are right some can cause decay. High temperatures and damaged skin let infection seep in and profits run out. Low temperature and ginger handling will keep the skin intact and good-looking and the microbes where you want them—on the surface.

Tactful signs may keep the pinchers, the pokers, and the strippers—a talented bunch of unknowing destroyers—from helping your microbial enemies steal freshness. "Keep our produce fresh for you; one touch can spoil. A squeeze can ruin perfect fruit." "Let us strip the corn for you—indecent exposure ravishes Nature's beautiful works," or something else could help. Letting customers bag their own purchases may save you time and work but it can give you real trouble in a high proportion of spoiled goods. People just can't realize that each of them inflicting one invisible bruise can ruin much produce over the day, making heavy losses for you. It's a problem no one has ever really solved—keeping inquisitive fingers off the merchandise and in the pocketbook. Direct criticism, though, is likely to make some people huffy. After all, they want to know what they're paying for. With quiet persuasion you'll offend no one and the food will be intact for the one who'll pay without a pinch.

Harvest when ready. Knowledge that you need to operate successfully (but can't get except gradually by experience) is how to be sure that fruits and vegetables are perfectly ready to harvest. Unripe melons, pears and tomatoes, harvested as the big and distant grower does it, can't ripen to their best flavor. Worse still, if you or the customer refrigerate them, the tomatoes especially, they are sure never to fill out their flavor, though it's the flavor that people buy them for. Tomatoes and also pears grown outside the regular season (as in hothouses) need temperature conditioning even more than the regular crop does.

Keep it moist. Produce that you can't refrigerate (either because you don't have a cooler or it hasn't room enough), needs help desperately in summer heat. It's called *moisture conditioning,* and it is meant to keep living things from losing their moisture, which causes wilting and shriveling. Most fruits and vegetables inside their cells are something like 80 to 85 per cent water. The spaces between those cells stay at nearly 100 per cent humidity—life-sustaining water. But if you leave the produce out in air that has less humidity than it needs to keep going, you're risking spoilage. The choice is either to refrigerate or to keep the air moist and the produce as cool as you can—moisten the fruits and vegetables directly.

A greenhouse will hold a lot of moisture, but is impractical for selling. Instead, when you display corn and other green produce, ice it and sprinkle it. Just watch how fast moisture on the surface evaporates. It has to be replaced as fast as it disappears to do any good. A fine sprayer will help on open and refrigerated displays, anything that isn't packaged.

Use ice. For non-refrigerated displays, chopped ice is good. You can apply it in several ways. A solid bed of ice on which you put the items you're displaying is the first. The second kind is channels of ice run between commodities. Either of these also can be combined with top garnishing, some ice spread over the produce. Unfortunately, any of these techniques has to be tended to continually to do any good. If you want to invest in it you can get a commercial ice channel, which gives ribbons of ice 3 by 7 inches spread 18 to 24 inches apart. This machine adds humidity and lowers the temperature to 40 or 45 degrees Fahrenheit, helping the produce hold 92 to 94 per cent of its weight in 72 hours; it also uses up electricity. Flat beds of ice of course do not send the cold all the way through the produce, but if you spread ice on top early in the morning (before opening up for the day), the produce will take up the moisture and will look (and be) fresh for the new day's selling. Ice bed displays need garnishing with more ice on top during the day—otherwise you'll lose 10 per cent of the produce even sitting on ice. It deteriorates noticeably, and you can't afford that.

Refrigeration is the best way of holding the quality built into your produce. With it, you carry the food over slow days, when it might otherwise be wasted altogether. Any kind of refrigeration, remember, is meant to slow the rate of respiration, the plant's breathing. That's vital because the plant doubles its rate for every 18 degrees the temperature climbs above 32 degrees Fahrenheit. Lowering the temperature even to 40 or 50 degrees will keep most produce in salable shape for three or four days. Tuck a thermometer in your shirt pocket and check everything at least once a day, never relying wholly on air temperature or a reading on the surface of a product. Stick the thermometer at least 2½ inches into an apple, a melon, or a head of lettuce near the center of a crate or display, and also near the middle of the vegetable or fruit. Leave it there for a few minutes, then take your reading and look at the table. Give the temperature very little leeway; if it's getting close to the dangerline, dress with ice or swap produce between display and cooler.

Cool power. With electricity so costly and going up, an old-time root cellar could come in very handy now. It used to do a perfectly good job for some fruits and vegetables.

With some kind of cooler in your market, you can move all perishables in there at night. That cooling will last well into the next day, unless it gets up to the high end of the glass. (That's when you realize how shade trees earn their keep.) Over the 24 hours on a summer's day the produce stored for the night at 40 degrees will be 20 degrees lower. That can add a day's shelf life for ripe apricots, artichokes, beans, broccoli, Brussels sprouts, cabbage, carrots, cauliflower, corn, endive, grapes, lettuce, mushrooms, parsnips, peas, ripe pears, plums, radishes or yellow and Italian squash. A day saved on held-over produce makes a noticeable difference in profits earned by not throwing these things into the garbage or compost heap.

By the way, if ice is easy to get where you are, or you make it yourself, an ice bed with ice covering the produce can give you results nearly as good as you'd get by moving everything to a cooler.

Cool corn. If much of your income depends on sweet corn, Roger Ginder of the University of Delaware suggests, it may be wise to refrigerate it, though you do sacrifice the appealing open bulk displays with big bins full of unhusked corn. Refrigerated cases cut the visibility and touchability that piles of corn have. But they will knock your losses to spoilage way down.

Ginder tells of other ways in which you can keep corn breathing:

(1) Pick the day's crop early in the morning before heat builds in the fields. It will need less cooling to stay at a healthy temperature.

(2) Keep all produce out of direct sunlight—always.

(3) Pick just enough for the day's selling, not a big amount every other day. The less it lies around separated from its source of life, the plant, the better it will be. ˙

(4) Do the same with corn that you have to buy from other growers, taking small lots often, not a larger lot once a week; also try to arrange it so that they will pick in the early hours.

(5) If you have to truck the corn in, cover it with ice for the trip.

(6) Also ice it in your displays.

(7) Display only a little and refrigerate the rest.

When you've done all that human wisdom can do to keep life in your produce, be ready to catch it before too much time passes and get it into your quick-sale display while it's still a good value.

PRODUCE QUALITY CONTROL

Item	Best Temperature	Freezing Point	Preferred Humidity (%)	Sprinkling	Quality Characteristics
Apples	32-35°F	28.5	85-90	None	Colorful, uniform, bruise-free
Apricots	32-35°	29.3	85-90	None	Plump, firm
Artichokes	32-35°	29.6	90-95	Lightly	Bright color, firm
Asparagus	32-35°	30.5	85-90	Lightly	Wilt-free, uniform
Avocados, unripe	65-75°	30.0	85-90	None	
ripe	40-50°	30.0	85-90	None	Smoothness, bruise-free
Bananas, unripe	65-75°	30.0	85-90	None	
ripe	55-60°	30.0	85-90	None	Uniform, mold-free, bright color
Beans, snap	45-50°	30.2	85-90	Lightly	Crisp, uniform, immature
lima	32-35°	30.9	85-90	Yes	Clean, well-filled, dark green
Beets	32-35°	30.5	80-90	Yes	Small, smooth, firm
Berries	32-35°	30.3	85-90	None	Bright, clean, plump
Broccoli	32-35°	30.5	90-95	Lightly	Cloud buds, clean, dark green
Brussels sprouts	32-35°	30.2	90-95	Yes	Hard, clean, compact
Cabbage	32-35°	30.5	90-95	Yes	Hard, heavy, bright color
Carrots	32-35°	28.7	90-95	Lightly	Firm, uniform, well-colored
Cauliflower	32-35°	30.2	85-90	Lightly	White, clean, compact curd
Celery	32-35°	30.9	90-95	Yes	Medium size, crisp, colorful
Cherries	32-35°	27.4	80-90	None	Bright, plump
Collards	32-35°	30.2	90-95	Yes	Fresh, immature, colorful
Corn	32-35°	29.9	85-90	Yes	Bright, plump, milky kernels
Cranberries	40-50°	29.7	85-90	None	High luster, firm, plump

Cucumbers	40-50°	36.7	85-95	None	Green, well-shaped, firm
Dates	32-35°	-0.4	70-75	None	Golden brown, slightly moist
Eggplant	40-50°	30.3	85-90	Yes	Heavy, rich color, scar
Endive-escarole	32-35°	30.9	90-95	Lightly	Fresh, immature, colorful
Figs	32-35°	30.0	85-90	None	Fairly soft, uniform
Grapefruit	32-60°	28.3	85-90	None	Springy touch, heavy
Grapes	32-35°	27.5	85-90	None	Plump, mature, fresh
Kale	32-35°	30.7	90-95	Yes	Fresh, immature, colorful
Leeks	32-35°	30.3	90-95	Yes	Fresh, uniform, clean
Lemons	40-50°	29.1	85-90	Lightly	Bright, heavy, fine texture
Lettuce	32-35°	31.0	90-95	Lightly	Clean, crisp, tender
Limes	45-50°	28.4	85-90	Yes	Firm, green, heavy
Mangoes	55-60°	29.4	85-90	None	Smooth, speckled, solid
Melons, unripe	55-60°	29.9	85-90	None	
ripe	40-50°	29.9	85-90	None	Mature, fine texture
Mushrooms	32-35°	30.1	90-95	None	Clean, white, wilt-free
Nectarines, unripe	65-75°	30.0	85-90	None	
ripe	32-35°	30.0	85-90	None	Plump, well colored, firm
Okra	40-50°	28.6	85-90	None	Clean, 2-4", fresh
Onions, dry	65-75°	30.2	70-75	None	Hard, bright, dry
green	32-35°	30.1	90-95	Lightly	Green, fresh, clean, uniform
Oranges	32-35°	28.5	85-90	None	Firm, heavy for size
Parsnips	32-35°	29.8	90-95	Yes	Smooth, clean, medium size
Peaches, unripe	65-75°	29.5	85-90	None	
ripe	32-35°	29.5	85-90	None	Bright, fresh, yellow background
Peas	32-35°	30.5	85-90	Lightly	Tender, young, sweet
Pears, unripe	60-70°	27.8	90-95	Lightly	
ripe	32-35°	27.8	90-95	None	Firm, unbroken skin, wilt-free

Item	Best Temperature	Freezing Point	Preferred Humidity (%)	Sprinkling	Quality Characteristics
Peppers	40-50°	30.5	85-90	Lightly	Fresh, green color, firm
Persimmons	32-35°b	27.5	85-90	None	Resemble plump, ripe tomato
Pineapple, unripe	65-75°	29.8	85-90	None	
ripe	40-50°	29.8	85-90	None	Golden yellow, "piney" aroma
Plums, prunes	32-35°b	29.0	85-90	None	Full colored, plump, slightly soft
Potatoes	65-75°c	30.0	85-90	None	Smooth, sound, firm
Pumpkins	55-60°	29.9	85-90	None	Hard, blemish free
Radishes	32-35°	30.1	90-95	Yes	Mild, bright, smooth
Rhubarb	32-35°	30.7	90-95	Yes	Crisp, bright, stout
Shallots	32-35°	31.6	90-95	Yes	Green, fresh tops
Spinach	32-35°	31.3	90-95	Yes	Fresh, immature, colorful
Squash, summer	40-50°	30.0	90-95	Lightly	Crisp, heavy, tender
winter	55-60°	29.8	85-90	None	Hard, blemish free
Sweet potatoes	55-60°	29.3	85-90	None	Bright, solid, well shaped
Tangerines	32-35°	29.5	90-95	Lightly	Deep color, heavy
Tomatoes, unripe	60-70°	30.6	85-90	None	
ripe	40-50°	30.8	85-90	None	Plump, bruise-free, firm, uniform red color
Turnips	32-35°	29.8	90-95	Yes	Heavy, smooth, firm
Watermelons	32-75°	30.5	85-90	None	Mature, well shaped

b: ripe   c: new crops 50°F

PESTS EAT PROFITS

Flies, fruit flies, beetles and other forms of wildlife that interest entomologists make a very bad impression on customers who spot them in residence around your market. But persistent as they seem and endless in their breeding, they can be controlled. The first, most important and easiest step is to take away from them whatever it is that encourages them to breed—like their favorite foods and dirt in the corners. Put vegetable trimmings and decayed produce into tightly covered garbage cans, removing them often to wherever it is safe and legal to dispose of them. If the refuse is to go into compost, keep it far away from the market or you may get more pests than you had before. Any harvests that have infested produce, such as corn with sap beetles, must be kept out of the market. Watch your fruit closely so that you can cull it as it ripens. Honeybees, indispensable as they are for pollinating and making honey, love ripe fruit, but customers like them not a bit. Even if the people aren't allergic to the sting, fear of it will put them off.

Pesticides. Chemical pesticides are challenged by almost everyone today, and with the best of reasons. They can kill the bugs they're meant for but they can turn on the bugs' enemy, too—you. And bugs can get to like them. But a pyrethrin spray once a week at closing time will get to all the corners, and without creating a big health problem, if you cover all the food. Pay no attention to the bug fryers that go pop when one lands on the electrified surface. They may be a curiosity, but they aren't especially attractive to people and do seem to draw more pests than you had before.

Bug lights spaced around the market outside are helpful at night, though they don't cure the trouble. Keeping weeds down around the market won't hurt, either. The few insects that get in through often-opened doors won't be a great bother.

As for using pesticides in your fields, some people say you can't stay in business without them; others that they wouldn't be caught dead spraying their plants. They're afraid of residual poisons—and I don't blame them. Until the research people come up with a safe substitute for pesticides, like chemical attractants made from the bug's own juices, be extremely careful in applying anything, getting guidance from your extension service.

Specific suggestions for the battle of the bug may add to your arsenal. David L. Matthews, professor of entomology at Purdue University, and Charles Williams, in *Insect Control at the Farm Market,* came up with the following and Ransom A. Blakeley has passed on the full discussion. They remind us of a new problem: Where people used to look for quality and appearance, they now want pesticide-free produce—*but* it must also be bug-free.

The best way of not having bugs is to be sure the market is clean. For that you need an effective sanitation program. If bugs do invade your market, you should know something about their life cycle so that you can clobber them with the best treatment at the right time. And to be sure you get control over them before they take over the business, you must have as much information about safe pesticides as you can come by.

Which bugs? The types of insects you are most likely to have are cockroaches (also known by a politer name, water beetles), ants, crickets, ground beetles, grain moths, picnic beetles, paper wasps, yellowjackets and the most familiar pest of all, flies. The picnic beetles can be baited away from the market. Yellowjackets are attracted to overripe fruit, which suggests one obvious treatment: remove fruit that's past its prime. And sanitation will cure the fly disease if you persist with it, especially by keeping animal manure distant from the market.

Insecticides. The types of bug-killing materials are almost as numerous as the bugs, though the Environmental Protection Agency has strictly narrowed their number and the ways in which you can apply them. We have insecticides, but we also have fungicides, herbicides, avicides, and rodenticides. These others we'll leave for another time. The residual types of insecticides good for the market's outside are *Diazinon, Kerlan, Cygon,* and *Malathion.* They are residual in that they stay around doing their killing for a while, but nowhere near as long as the almost-eternal DDT and *Dieldrin. Malathion* is shortest-lived and probably safest for that reason, but it's effective while it lasts.

A good program (if any insecticide can be called good), is to apply *Malathion* and *Diazinon* to the outside walls every four to eight weeks, if you have to. You can also use these inside before the season starts and before you have any produce on display. The aerosol bombs that can be useful in clearing a building of bugs are in bad trouble. Or they will be soon if a final study verifies that the fluorocarbon gas that powers some of them then rises to the upper atmosphere and breaks down the ozone up there.

Most pesticides approved for use inside have *pyrethrin* in them. That is made from a chrysanthemum relative grown in Kenya. It knocks down flies on contact, but there is the end of its service—it is not residual. Always cover produce and food-handling counters with plastic sheet to keep the spray off—it isn't good for people.

The yellow plastic strips that you see hung around many markets hold a chemical called DDVP, *Vapora* or *dichlorvos.* The vapor it gives off kills flies *inside* the market. Outside it does no good. But it isn't good for people on their food, and so should be used only in storage areas where no food is kept.

Food preparation. One very important function that needs constant management in any market is preparation. It usually begins, if the produce is your own, with a good cleaning of every piece of produce. Some people may prefer to eat the food as it comes from tree, vine or ground; and others will ask if they should wash it first. Clean everything that grows in or on the ground, and certainly any crops that were sprayed. Have all produce looking and tasting neat as well as fresh and ripe. Trimming is a matter of taste for most vegetables. But pulling off the lettuce's outer leaves when they are yellowed, beet greens for separate sale, and any other preparatory steps that seem necessary—these are common sense.

GRADE FOR QUALITY AND SALES

Most markets do grading of some kind, keeping it much more informal than the commercial markets do. And most customers seem to prefer merchandise that is separated into at least two qualities—good and best. The broad grades that the state and federal regulatory agencies set up for many products are helpful if you use them; your own sense of what customers consider good buys is usually enough, as long as you comply with legal standards and don't advertise grades different from those you sell. For the latest grading standards, write to the Fruit and Vegetable Division, Consumer and Marketing Service, USDA, Washington, D.C. Some grading is good for customers because it tells them that they are getting dependable quality in their produce. It also can help marketers, because it adds some variety in the sizes, qualities, and therefore the prices they can offer to a public that is of many minds. Both the customers who are out for quality regardless of price and the bargain-hunters are pleased to have a choice.

How is grading done? It depends on whether or not you follow the USDA standards. Some people start by examining every unit of each kind of produce, checking size, quality, color, condition, and anything else that could affect the eating quality. Following the USDA descriptive grades means giving very close attention to the specifications. You probably won't want to get involved in such details as figuring out the differences (as you hold a pear in your hand) between U.S. Extra Fancy, U.S. Fancy, U.S. Extra Number 1, and U.S. Number 2. One or two grades seems enough, the second grade being reserved for quick-sale merchandise. But it's an education to study the full range of grades a little.

Packaging. Most small operators avoid the cost and trouble that anything but the simplest packaging can get them into. Going too far in that direction can hoist you to the big-market class, a move that not many people choose to make. About the only packaging that's really needed is the box or carton that berries are put in, or the bag, box, or carton that you may want to put fruit in for convenience, quicker sale, or more consistent quantities. Berries do need much care, as do fancy fruits that bring high prices. Packaging manufacturers aren't hard to find. You may go to one for bags, and while there you may learn as much as you need to know about the many other kinds of packaging you can choose to make life easier and more profitable, both for you and the customers. Even the cheapest container will send your cost for each unit of produce you sell up a little. But the profit you make on it may go up too, if you pick the packaging that will be appealing, protective, and convenient to handle. Having the market's name printed on the package is low-cost advertising that goes a long way. Each package will be a reminder of a good shopping experience to the customer who carried it home, and a suggestion to anyone else who sees it that your market may be worth a try. Some kinds of plastic packagings now seem unavoidable, because we've gotten used to their superior qualities and usefulness. Plastic, though, can give that unwanted commercial feeling, and it's undesirable when it gets to the dump, where it might last at least forever. Perhaps technology will find us a biodegradable plastic that will be cheap yet recyclable. Package when you have to; save money when you don't.

PRICING QUALITY

Packaging brings up another part of your job that isn't altogether controllable by common sense—every package or selling unit has to have a price. For pricing the packages, you may rely on a felt-tip marker or a crayon or a commercial rubber stamp. All three take time. Better is a simple price card on each display with the name of the product and the price for each unit. Making up a few signs is a lot quicker than marking hundreds of packages individually. It also makes changing prices effortless and cuts down on errors; the fewer times you have to mark a price, the less chance you have of making one of those trouble-provoking mistakes ("but it's *marked* a dozen for 50 cents, not six for a dollar").

Now for ideas on deciding which prices to choose. Many of these suggestions on pricing and markup I owe to those helpful specialists, Ransom A. Blakeley and Roger G. Ginder.

How to set prices. Any packaging and pricing policy you decide on at the beginning has to be stuck with: customers expect consistency here as in quality. How do marketers decide which prices will go on each item of produce? Where do you find out (1) how much the traffic will bear, and (2) how high a price you have to charge to make a profit? You could simply go around to see what everyone else is charging and pick that figure or push it up or down a little. Soon enough you'll find which price is right for keeping the customers coming. But let's be systematic about this profitable subject, and look at Roger Ginder's suggestions for finding the markup you need.

You can take your production cost or the wholesale price and add on your own markup, maybe ending up between the supermarket price and the wholesale figure, give or take a few pennies. Take a few if the quality in your produce is markedly better than what you see on someone else's shelves. Give some to bring people looking for a bargain *if* your costs can stand the cut. Expecting quite a high volume? Then you can knock off a little, still pulling in a fair profit. Consider your location. Will it be too much of a strain for people to travel to you, only to find prices no lower than they would pay anywhere else, or even higher? Where many customers seem likely to be richer or poorer than average, use that knowledge in gauging the margin. Marketers in the University of Maine study found that most of their customers make $10,000 to $20,000 a year, which can mean that many people who are not so well off stick to markets in the cities, probably paying dearly for the convenience though they can least afford it. It may also be a hint that the people going to markets in the country are more conscious of quality and less worried about price. Matching prices with the competition can take you in one of two directions. With other marketers charging on the high side for everything, you might want to go along; you can always knock prices down later.

That choice can be chancy, though. Let people get the idea that your market is the one with really good fruits and vegetables, but noticeably high prices, and you may never be able to shake off the expensive image. You could lose the customers who have modest ideas about what they can afford to spend on fresh food. Certainly, though, prices a bit higher than the supermarkets get may be okay if you give fine service on top of solid quality and a warm welcome. What kinds of service? We'll come back to that in Chapter 9.

Pricing sense. Be careful to apply a full measure of common sense in choosing which prices to keep high. Staple products, says Silas B. Weeks, Extension Economist at the University of New Hampshire, among them potatoes, have to be priced competitively—not a lot higher than supermarket prices, even if it means keeping your margin down on these items. That encourages people to buy more of your staple items and save themselves another stop on their shopping trip. For the roadside specialities that are best freshly picked, like corn, prices can be more flexible—you can charge more than the big markets do because they can't

compete with your fresh, high quality. Prices also have to be aimed at volume. It's hard to get away with carrying all high-priced merchandise. Some few customers don't give a fig about high prices if they get unusual value. Another small percentage of the people who come to you are the sharp bargain hunters who care little for perfection in foods. Between the spenders and the savers are most of the customers, the ones who make your sales volume. To attract and keep them, your markup has to be reasonable. Compromise to hit the golden mean.

Demand—the other hard-to-fathom side of the pricing equation—depends on how much *your* customers are willing to pay for *your* product. Blakeley gives eggplants as an example. If you decide that (1) your customers can't get fresh eggplants, (2) you can produce and sell them for a decent price, and (3) you have enough customers who want eggplants so much that they will pay a premium price for them, then go ahead and produce eggplants and charge a handsome price.

Instead of fighting with your competitors for the limited satisfaction you might get from a price war, improve your service, your advertising, or your product so that customers will realize *your* deal is better than anyone else's, and they will be willing to buy even if the price tells them they shouldn't.

Count your costs. Know your costs of production; both your variable costs—what it will cost to produce this item this year—and your fixed costs. Once you know these, you can figure out your total cost for producing that crop. Because your costs and your yields are different from anyone else's, only you can work out these costs. The work is not too wearisome. An hour to an hour and a half is enough to spend arriving at the cost for producing one crop.

The marketing costs have to be figured in, too: investment in the building, taxes, display fixtures, lighting for nighttime selling, heat for cool months, electricity for refrigeration and lights, cost for hired employees, materials for packaging, and all the rest. Separate records (marked Market) are the only way to keep track of these costs.

All this is part of putting a rational foundation under your prices—why charge this for that? You can, of course, set the figures arbitrarily, though that is improvident. *Markup* is the method any successful marketer uses to make sure he stays in business. Working from your unit cost—the amount you spend on overhead, including building construction, mortgage, rent, depreciation, cultivating, preparing, and selling—you add to each item you have for sale a specific proportion, to pay all the costs and to give you a profit. By choosing the right figure you can be sure that your prices will be neither too fat to draw people nor shaved too close to the breakeven point, where you make less than a reasonable profit, or none.

Profit margin. One mistake may trap you if you don't watch for it. Roger Ginder reminds that taking a percentage of your cost for producing an item (or buying it if you don't grow it) will give you a smaller figure than you get by working backward from your selling price for the item. Let's say it costs you $1 for so much of an item and your accustomed markup is 20 per cent of the sales price; your price will then be $1.25. In other words, pick your price by the considerations mentioned here, then figure your margin from that price. Simply taking a percentage of the higher figure (the selling price) instead of the lower (the unit cost) gives you a higher profit. If the margin is excessively high when you take it from the selling price, you know that price is too high, or maybe the margin should be lower on that one item to reduce the price and increase the item's attractiveness. Conversion scales like the one reproduced here are handy for figuring markups. Try your county agent for other variations.

Units or multiples? In setting up your pricing practices, how will you assign prices to the *quantities* you sell? Will you choose unit pricing, charging one price for each unit, no matter how big the purchase—so much a bunch, or 90 cents a box, or 10 cents apiece, or so much a pound? Or is the multiple pricing system best for you: 50 cents a pound and 90 cents for two pounds of this, one head of that for 30 cents and two heads for 50 cents? Or so much for a bunch, a little less than

CONVERSION SCALE FOR MARKUP
BY COST AND SALES

Choose in the right-hand column the percentage of sales value that you feel is necessary to cover all your costs above the purchasing price or cost of producing your merchandise. The profit that you desire as a percentage of gross sales should also be included in this percentage markup. You then multiply the percentage value from the left column by the cost of the item, giving you the approximate markup on sales needed to maintain the margin you want.

Markup on Costs		*On Sales*
15%	equals about	13%
18%	equals about	15%
20%	equals about	18%
25%	equals about	20%
30%	equals about	23%
33%	equals about	24%
34%	equals about	25%
35%	equals about	26%
40%	equals about	29%
44%	equals about	30%
50%	equals about	33%
54%	equals about	35%
60%	equals about	38%
65%	equals about	40%

(From *Guidelines to Successful Roadside Marketing* by C. W. Porter, Special Circular 70, College of Agriculture Extension Service, Pennsylvania State University, University Park, Pennsylvania.)

twice that much for double the amount? Roger Ginder says multiple pricing sells larger quantities and makes the produce seem cheaper. The unit price you have in mind stays the same—it's just easier to sell larger quantities.

The missing cent. Then decide if you'll go in for the commercial-looking pricing by "nines"—$1.49 for two pounds. That missing penny, some believe, makes the difference between selling or not selling—the price that's just under 50 cents or a dollar or two dollars is supposed to convince customers that you've cut the price to the core. Or, to hold the honest, informal image that can be very important to thoughtful people, price by fives and tens. That also makes totting up prices easier for customers and you: 55 cents a dozen and $1.05 for two dozen. Avoiding the nines will save handling pennies, too, and copper is scarce.

Ginder says of multiple pricing that it can help you move overstocked produce, that reducing the price a little for multiple-unit purchases beats lowering all the unit prices, and that it is a legitimate merchandising practice. It encourages bigger purchases, too. It does seem insulting to the public's intelligence to believe that a penny's difference will push them over the line of conviction. And if marking something 99 cents a pound seems silly, it gets worse as the price grows, all the way to a car going for $3,999. No one could arrive at a price like that without a scrap of deception in mind.

Price consistently. Joseph F. Hauck, extension and research specialist on marketing at Rutgers University, has a suggestion that reinforces the idea we've seen already. He warns against revising your prices every day to keep them in line with whatever sources of price comparison you follow (wholesalers, other farm markets, or supermarkets). That gives you more work than you need and makes your pricing policy look jumpy and inconsistent. Customers may react in the wrong way, thinking you're as interested in that last penny as the big marketer. You need their confidence, and you could lose it unless you set up a steady, reliable price structure, even though your prices may not be the lowest around.

Price lining may help. Have two lines of prices just for your major items. Sort out imperfect but edible fruit and vegetables with noticeable but harmless imperfections and price them much lower than your best quality. Customers can *choose* to buy the lower-priced line instead of having to go to your competitor to pay less; it also convinces them they are saving money.

Here's another thought: Produce a product to meet a demand, instead of producing the cheapest merchandise people will accept. And then build that demand. Advertise by variety: "We have *Wonderful* or *Sweet Sue* or *Gold Cup,*" means a lot more than the supermarket advertiser's fancy adjective thinly disguising aged ears of corn. And you might leave prices out of your ads—why compete directly with the supermarketer who has cheaper food for lower prices? The nickel pricing, too, makes a solid figure for the customer to deal with—no hint of the bargain-basement or cheap merchandise.

Ransom Blakeley also says to *evaluate* your pricing. Is a product moving faster (or slower) because of price, or for some other reason? It could be price, and low volume can be a sign of that. Or it could be the package that's hiding the product, or a big display hiding a smaller one, or a hundred other mistakes. At least if the price is too low, you'll know it. You'll just keep running out.

Know city prices. To charge all that people will pay, know the prices wholesalers are charging. Following the city wholesalers' prices regularly will show you how much retailers in general are willing to pay for their produce. The federal or state departments of agriculture in many cities put out a weekly fresh fruit and vegetable report with wholesale prices, and information on quality, size, and condition of produce. Some even will report to you by telephone or by mail. These prices are a base from which you can figure your markup. Once you have a feeling for the price range covered by other roadside marketers, nearby supermarkets, and the city wholesalers, you can think about your own costs of production and selling, the markup you'll have to tack on, and the pricing policy that will keep your market solvent.

Should prices show? Should you mark prices at all, or give them only when the customer asks? Some marketers firmly believe that pricing all their produce so that all can see is a giveaway—it may scare people off (unless the charges are low compared with what they are used to paying). These marketers feel that being asked an item's price gives them an opening for a little sales pitch.

Most customers seem to expect clearly marked prices, having been trained in the supermarkets that everything is usually obviously priced, even to the unit of weight or volume. Quality there may be overlooked, but you get used to that when you feed your family an all-supermarket diet. The same customers who have to ask what you charge sometimes feel funny if your price sounds too high for them, though they hesitate to say "No thank you," just because the price is beyond their reach.

Doesn't it seem fairest to get your prices out in the open, with no apologies? Then the customer has time to think before choosing an item, comparing and making mental notes on how good your produce looks, and how the prices really aren't as high as they seemed at first. Anyway, instead of spending a lot of time quoting prices, you might better put the time into constructive selling. The semi-self-service approach isn't the worst. Even if it means boxing or bagging things in advance and marking the price on every container, there won't be any bickering. You'll save selling time and labor, and behold, the customers may sell themselves much of the time. Take a leaf from the big marketer's book and display your prices.

Chapter 5
Workers

No matter how small your market is when you start out, you might find that the day gets long, customers gang up on you, and profits don't rise as fast as the amount of business you're doing says they should. A classic farm market, staffed by family alone—yourself when you have time from the gardening or farming, your wife or husband, the children old enough to help, and a close relative or two—ought to keep you in fine shape for a while. But the growing business may take more hands. Plenty of marketers prefer to stay with that practical system, but others find growth more tempting. They are the ones who must be wholly businesslike. For them, the question isn't to hire or not, but hire how many? Some larger markets that are run by families take in relatives well beyond the usual family circle, and from several generations. When it is time to go outside for help, you will meet surprises and all will not be joyful. Finding, paying, and handling hired help can be an ever-growing nuisance. With talent for managing people, though, you may find the added pressure more fun than bother.

MANY HANDS

How much help will you need? At the season's peak, business may be so rushed that people don't get waited on, stock runs out faster than you can replenish it just when the crowd is at its biggest, and the market may get messy with no one having time to clean up.

In hiring as everywhere else, small is the way to start; even one part-timer may make the difference. Happily, the height of the summer season comes in school vacation when all kinds of bright, capable, and eager people want work. It's hard to say just where to start looking for the most helpful and reliable workers. High schoolers, college students, retired people, all can be of great service to you. If you can get along with a part-time helper, you might do better hiring someone older, whose only limitations may be strength or weariness from long hours of standing.

Be demanding. Hiring young or old, you'll have to be demanding about qualifications, even when help is scarce, if your workers are to help in the selling. They will represent you and your market and they must add to its attractiveness and efficiency. For dealing with the public, pick only those who are personable, who make friends easily, and who are not put off quickly by unpleasantness in the public's behavior. Taking punishing words and holding the tongue can be more important than documented selling experience, great intelligence, or striking salesmanship. Courtesy, neat appearance, and a fair amount of enthusiasm will make the good impression that is all the customers get much of the time. The important, deeper qualities such as reliability count more for you as an employer. Always ask for and check references, even if you are a good judge of people. Naturally, everyone will give names of people most likely to be on his side and not necessarily unbiased, but some direct questions, if answered directly, will give you valuable confirmation about plus and minus qualities. Remember to take both praise and blame with salt.

TRAINING PAYS OFF

To be of good service in helping to run the market, a new worker has to know quite a lot that can be learned only from you. Train any helper, including people in your family, in salesmanship, handling people, knowledge of your product, and money matters. Some people will pick up knowledge like this almost at the first mention, but most will need some practice on the job before they are good at it.

Tell them something about how you grow your crops and the time, effort, skill, and cost that it takes to produce food successfully. No, it's not easier than it looks—it's a lot harder. Give them a good short course about competition in your area, including prices, the advantages and disadvantages of your produce compared with what people will find in other markets. To back you up effectively they should know the reasons for your ways of doing business. And they must have a very clear statement from you on working hours, salary, overtime, and responsibilities. Spell everything out, then any misunderstandings that come up can be settled by a reminder, not a reprimand.

The more the people working for you know about efficient ways of running the business, the more likely each is to bring in far more than enough business to cover the salary—a healthy share of productivity.

Choose people who will handle more than one kind of work, and more work than the minimum they can get away with. One good choice in hiring may bring twice as much productivity as two mediocres, meaning you can get along with fewer extra hands. Self-starters also need less supervision, giving you more time to spend on managing and planning.

Set up rules. Roger G. Ginder's training ideas include getting something on paper for people's guidance—not just hired people but family too. They should have a full list of things they must know and all their responsibilities:

(1) Handling disputes and customers and returned merchandise starts the list, and it may be the most vital thing anyone can learn in dealing with the public. No, the customer *isn't* always correct. But there's a trick in getting them not to mind having you point out that they're wrong. When someone has misunderstood something (and that's the heart of most arguments), a clear explanation should straighten it out.

(2) Become an expert on how to make a sale, from opening remark to writing down amounts and prices for every item on a sales slip (or punching them into the cash register), to announcing the total price, to bagging or boxing it all neatly and conveniently, to the questions "Could you use some tree-ripened XXX?—right at their peak this week," to helping carry large purchases, and the final "Thank you, come see us again, please."

(3) Be sure everyone understands who is to clean up the market during the selling day and at the end of the day, to prepare the market for opening in the morning and closing at night, and to shut it down before a day off.

(4) Be explicit about promptness in starting work, specifying the usual hours, and mention that overtime will be expected and paid for, and that it will come at unpredictable times—any time at all.

(5) Be sure everyone knows who will stock the displays the night before, in the morning, and during the day.

(6) Show helpers how to handle produce—using the gentle touch—and the ways of keeping it in good condition.

(7) Emphasize the importance of attitude toward fellow workers and customers—cooperation and friendly straightforwardness.

(8) Be sure everyone knows who's in charge at all times, whether you're handy or not.

A list like this can be worked up into a book-length course in how to handle a job, but a page or two should be enough. Although no one can cover everything that's going to come up, spend the time to make sure that all the rules are clear and on paper. Rules must, of course, be bendable, built with reasonable areas of flexibility; all that matters is that they are there for everyone to see. Cover the most important things you can imagine happening, with general statements, yet put in enough detail to make them clear and strong enough to rebut obvious arguments. People (especially young ones) say they detest rules, but discipline is one of the things that people and businesses can't live without. Then too, anyone working for you represents *you* before the public. To keep them from misrepresenting you, train them.

Keep the list short, for the people who have a tiny span of attention and an even shorter memory. Above all, no matter how slight the rules seem, make them stick. That may be harder to do with people in your own family than with strangers, but it's for everyone's good.

Where are the workers? Once you have your ideas on how to handle helpers, you can set about finding willing workers. Probably the best source is that old friendly word of mouth. Naturally it doesn't always turn out that someone else's opinion is best for you. Yet you can cut out a few unknowns when you take leads from someone well known to you or your friends or neighbors. Ask people whose standards for people and honesty are as high as yours; casting about among strangers isn't likely to catch the best helpers.

Probably the place to start asking is at your county agent's office; do it some months before you'll need the people. Here again, planning early cuts later trouble. Gather on paper all the qualifications you are looking for, the number of helpers you'll need, how many hours they'll be expected to work, how much you expect to pay and the kinds of work you need done. If this source doesn't turn up helpers in a reasonable time, try local colleges or high schools. Remember, it's almost impossible to get someone who's overqualified to be a helper. You can't be too intelligent or too well educated, though someone who isn't very bright or has too little schooling is less than desirable. College placement offices, guidance counsellors, and teachers can be very helpful. Talk to the candidates directly as soon as you can.

Be choosy. You needn't be as demanding as if you were looking for a lifetime partner, but it's wasteful to spend time considering anyone who doesn't come up to the minimum qualifications we just went over. Snap decisions are worse than none; the first person you talk to may sound just about perfect, but the next in line may be even better. If you've started looking early enough, you should have time to choose the best possible workers. High unemployment may offer you really willing and able people whom you wouldn't have a chance at in easier times. Think about each candidate overnight. When you're down to one or more candidates, you might introduce them to the people they'll be working with; impressions from people you know could be helpful.

If you find no one suitable from these direct sources, try putting an ad in the local paper, carefully worded to cover everything you expect to find in a prospect. It isn't easy to write a compact but thorough ad for the help-wanted column, but give it several tries before sending it to the paper. It will cost less (and perhaps bring quicker results) if you type the ads on 3-by-5-inch cards and pin them up on local bulletin boards at supermarkets, colleges, high schools, churches, and clubs. Don't neglect retired farmers and teachers or business men and women, who could bring many talents to your market. If you are trying for a part-time person, don't hire someone who is putting in a lot of hours on a full-time job or is doing other part-time work. There's such a thing as spreading one's energies too thin. Probably employment agencies should not be the first places you go to, even though these may specialize in farm help. True, public agencies won't charge anything, and they might get you some first-class people, but you're more likely to find the helpers you need from local sources you know better.

Youth and age. School-age kids may be your best helpers, but they're not always dependable until they get to college age or beyond. Some say that high school girls are better for this kind of work than the male of the breed. If you're thinking of the younger people, watch out for the very tight regulations the government applies to anyone employing minors, and the limitations on what they are allowed to do.

Going back to the retired people, you may know many who retired early, not by their own choice but because their companies decided young blood is better than old. These older people often are eager, to say the least, for a chance to beef up their incomes (social security or pension or both). If you can find someone who's done years of responsible work, especially selling to or otherwise facing the public, you're far ahead hiring him, whatever kind of work he has done before.

Older people may or may not be able to handle heavy work such as moving the produce around, and they may not stand up perfectly for hours on their feet. They also may have problems getting to and from work if they don't live close to your market.

Yet these possible defects, Roger Ginder says, may be far outweighed by the benefits they bring to you. Their working habits may be reinforced by years of self-discipline. You can expect that they are good at getting to work on time, put in consistently full days working, fritter away little time on unproductive matters, and take great pride in their work and in satisfying their employer and the customers. The humility nourished in handling life's problems and dealing with many kinds of people over the years can build up priceless good judgment and sensitivity to other people's desires, preferences, and difficulties.

Older folks are also likely to stick to a job longer and more happily than the sometimes less stable young people. And that is worth plenty to you. Retired people especially have fewer chances to move about and are inclined to be faithful. School kids very naturally are inclined to move often, either dissatisfied in general or eager to find other career work. Many of the elders, unlike younger workers, don't *have* to earn a living. They may take a job because they want to, not because necessity forces them to, which may mean they'll be pleased with smaller salaries. The incentives that drive them to do good work run much deeper than money—the fun in greeting people, doing something productive, being helpful to someone, and simply not vegetating. All these pluses, and a relaxed attitude toward life, can give your market the golden touch that age can bring.

How much to pay? Once you know who it is you want to hire and where to find them, prepare to talk money. That should be no great trouble unless you're looking for a full-time, professional worker, which most marketers aren't unless they get into big-time, commercial marketing. An hourly wage will satisfy most people, as long as it's at least the minimum wage. From someone better qualified, a salary plus commission or even commissions alone could draw the extra effort that will build their income and your market. Tacking a commission onto an hourly rate may make an employe more eager to be attentive to the public, missing no chance to use his skills. But for retired people or school kids, a straight salary, hourly or weekly, is likely to be the best arrangement.

Even if the part-time workers aren't covered by regulations such as the minimum wage law, offering only what the law allows means that you're probably not going to get the most helpful workers or the high productivity you're used to with family helpers. Decent pay also helps (but doesn't guarantee) happier workers; that mood can spread to the people they work with and to the customers, who will respond more positively than to glum clerks.

More red tape. Bookkeeping grows as your market does, and hiring can mound you over with paperwork. Payroll deductions for withholding tax, social security, health insurance, and other matters have to be tended religiously to supply the perfect records the governments demand. You may need help first in this area, and again a retired person may be just the experienced hand you need.

HOW TO SELL

Many smaller marketers think it is bad business to be a pushy salesman, acting like a big-company peddler. Part of the charm and the worth in the farm market is the idea that the public helps sell itself a worthy product offered by a respectable producer and marketer. Yet to make success, anyone who sells to the public must live up to standards.

You have to know the answers to all the usual questions people ask about your market and your product. That's not so hard as it may seem; with at least a few months or at most a couple of years' experience, you should have run into most of the questions that can come up. They reduce themselves to formulas, and so do the answers you'll get used to offering. For the rare questions that stump you, at least find out where to get an answer, simply by calling your county agent or agricultural school. It's vital to know your product inside and out, from seed to growing plant to market to storage to the uses people put it to. Knowing what to say, though, is no more important than being aware by instinct and practice *when* to say what—and when to say nothing at all.

There are encyclopedias full of things about sales-manship, as you can see in publishers' bottomless lists. And you might find simple and probably useful scraps of advice in a book or a course, if you haven't already learned them from your own common sense. Sensible selling is an act that convinces people they need something you have without their noticing what you are doing to convince them. It's psychology, and it's needed to back up the quality in your produce and the quantity in your service.

Impulse buying. You also can prove to them that they need something they didn't know they needed—a very important part of selling. Most of the things people buy they really needed (or wanted). Others they had no idea of buying, until they saw the products on display. The impulse hits and it is hard to convince them they *don't* want it or need it, if for some crazy reason you should want to dissuade them. That is *impulse buying,* and selling hasn't much to do with it. You could suggest everything in the market, one thing at a time, without adding a penny to a customer's purchases. But let them see things set out before them and something happens—sometimes. Other people at other times need to have an item shown to them and explained, virtue by virtue, because they really don't think they want or need it. For one kind of customer, all you have to do is hand over an article and collect the price, not getting in the way of the transaction by offering information and advice except when you're asked.

Selling talk. Another kind of customer takes more active talking by you—a few quiet suggestions, such as "Have you noticed these *very* fresh peas?" For the third type of customer, you'll have to be a bit more convincing: "These are the first of the season. Cook them five minutes, no more. They're more nourishing than canned peas and their flavor's far better than frozen kinds. Cook them with these tiny fresh-grown onions for a healthy, substantial side dish." Or, to sell a bigger quantity: "Try some of these in your freezer. Won't it be a welcome change to have your own fresh-frozen peas to put on the table in January, looking just as they do now? And the price is the lowest you'll find." (Because they're a few days old and not your top quality, you've marked them half off for just such a quick sale.)

Toss in a little humor if you know the customer well, but often funny remarks are just as likely to be met with a glower as a snicker. Customers' moods are impossible to predict.

One indispensable technique in selling is starting the conversation that may lead to a sale. This may seem unimportant when you think that in the Maine survey of roadside markets the average sale was only two dollars, which may well be typical for most markets. But every two-dollar sale counts—you can't afford to drop any. Starting with a cheery "May I help you?" could bring you a flat, no-nonsense "NO!" instead of breaking the ice. Try a friendly but quiet "Hi!" and see how that works. Even that might cost a customer in New England, where people expect to be left alone to make up their own minds. Try a favorable comment on something that a customer is looking at: "Look fresh, don't they? They're an hour off the vine. We've had good luck with those tomatoes this year. Every one of them looks like the prizewinner we had last year." Say no more.

Once you've got something said, and have some sign of interest in return, even if it's only a noncommittal grunt, don't press your advantage beyond the point of usefulness. People tire quickly of helpful, informative talk when it keeps them from concentrating on "Well, we can eat those tonight, but what about tomorrow night? I wonder if they don't cost less at that big market we passed a mile or so back."

Know when the best thing to do is let go, and move slowly off about your business, but not too far away. Conversation isn't useful any more when the subject has changed in the listener's mind; then it's an interruption. It takes plenty of practice to know when the mind will go click and the decision to buy is settled. When the customer is clearly ready to buy, know when *not* to press your luck by asking "Will one pound be enough? They go pretty fast with hungry kids around." Close the sale, not the conversation. If any doubt remains, you can kill the sale by pushing a little too hard, fattening an uncertainty into a "no."

Informative tact. You can turn selling into a game of wits, but why make your job tougher than it needs to be? A customer who dropped by for nothing more than a bunch of carrots should not have to face a debate. Tact (that means open mind, closed mouth) is the key that may open a lot of friends and closed purses. You can, when it feels appropriate, mention other things that go with an item well, or something that's at its peak this week, or something else that's a bargain because the harvest is getting close to its end, or a new crop that will be coming in tomorrow. Little truthful facts can convince if they're coated with explanations. Remember that even though everything may seem too obvious to mention, that's because you're so close to the work every day. Most people will know next to nothing about your produce, except how to prepare it when it's home in the kitchen.

KNOW YOUR PRODUCE

Knowledge gives you confidence and power over customers—power to help them while you sell your produce. The sooner you and your helpers can learn everything about the things you sell, the better you'll feel about offering them to the public and the more effectively you'll get them off your shelves and into the customer's home. Know all types of fruit and vegetables, even the ones you don't carry (so that you can explain why you don't), how long things can be kept in a refrigerator or out of it, whether things can be frozen and for how long, which things are best raw and with what sauces or dips, which go with which meats, how much to buy for two or four or six people, what needs to be washed, which are most nutritious, and which are best for people who have to think about their weight. Most knowledge like that will be needed by someone, though some people won't care about any of it.

Every item you sell should have its own short story, to be held for just the right moment. It might help, when you're training salespeople, to have a card written up with facts about each item, adding to it whenever you learn something timely. Of course, people working close together will pick up bits of information from each other and often from customers, who pass on useful information gleaned from other markets, books, radio, or television.

Sources of information. If your educational television channel has a program on gardening, cooking, and related subjects, watch it regularly. People will expect you to know the ideas already, but you could learn a lot. As a producer you can correct notions spread by people who may know about small gardens but maybe not about producing things in quantity. Expect to do quite a lot of homework like this, just as people in other professions must.

The farming and gardening magazines can help you keep up to date. *Farm Journal, Organic Gardening and Farming,* and others don't have to be read cover to cover. Skim them when you receive your issues or visit the library, or take notes from the articles that mean something. Keep up with the literature, and with all other sources of facts on your specialty.

A sample of the information you could put on a card:

```
Vegetable: lettuce
Variety: Iceberg
Uses: salads, alone or mixed with other greens, with
sliced or whole cherry tomatoes, spinach, cut-up
chives or scallions, sliced Bermuda onions, watercress,
sliced carrots, sliced apples, whole grapes, raisins,
crushed cooked bacon.
Dressings: vinegar alone, or salad oil plus vinegar,
or olive oil and vinegar (2:1 mixture) allowed to sit
at least overnight with 1 clove of crushed garlic,
small amounts (½ teaspoon or so) of oregano, thyme,
rosemary, and marjoram for each pint.
Freshness of dressing: keeps indefinitely without re-
frigeration if you use pure olive oil.
Keeping lettuce: lasts a week or more in refrigerator
crisper; can't be frozen.
Washing: usually none needed unless grown in very sandy
soil; if grower hasn't washed it, rinse whole head with
cold water spray.
```

THE ACT OF SELLING

You may want to prepare a complete procedure for trainees to learn to follow in selling. There are steps that should not be skipped, even though the seller and the customer may be busy and distracted.

Sales slips. If you use sales slips, write down each item in readable shorthand, then add up all and put down the total, meanwhile saying each item's name and price and the total, loud enough for the purchaser to hear. The same goes for punching the items into an adding machine or cash register. End by handing the sales slip, register tape with total, or adding machine tape to the customer, repeating the total to make sure both of you know what it is.

Money handling. Next take the customer's payment and put paper money on the counter next to adding machine or register or on the cash register's shelf; bills must *never* go directly into the cash drawer. Count all change, coins first, bills last, into the customer's hand, saying the amounts as you hand them over and mentioning the amount the customer gave you as well as the change you are giving back ($2.25 total out of $3.00; I owe you 75 cents). Handing all the change in a lump to the customer or slapping it down on the counter to be picked up awkwardly is just impolite and unacceptable, regardless of rush. Only when the customer has accepted the change you've counted out, completing the exchange between you, should you put the bills into the register or cash drawer.

Take simple precautions to reduce losses: For personal checks, mention the market's name or show it printed, to prevent mistakes. For new customers write the full name and address (if they aren't already printed on the check) on the back of the check, along with driver's license number or home phone number. Always ask for identification if a check is handed you, preferably a driver's license or charge card with the customer's signature, and write the charge card numbers on the back of the check. Always, too, have the customer write the check for the exact amount of the sale, not for some larger sum. Make sure the amount written on the check is the same in both places, and double-check it with the total on your register or adding machine or sales slip. For small errors the customer can correct the check by clearly writing out the amount and signing his initials next to the corrected figure. Last, see that the customer has signed the check—legible or not, a signature is necessary.

HANDLING PEOPLE

A few other ideas should enter into your sales conversations. Try politely to keep anyone—co-worker or fellow customer—from interrupting your interchange with each customer. If you are interrupted, say: "I'll be with you as soon as this customer has been served." That should be enough to hold off all but the rudest butters-in. But take a second to answer any brief, direct question—such as "Where are the eggs, please?"—but then continue quickly with the original customer. Leave any impolite questions or statements unresponded to until you've thought out the answer. Then say simply the things that are part of your formal procedure in making a sale. The quiet reminder that you want to serve the customer you're waiting on now should cut off the impatient.

Politeness. Be forgiving. Act as if the nasty remark had never been said. Keep track of the order in which customers came to you—nothing is worse than a dispute over who's next, drummed up by a curmudgeon, especially if you have taken someone out of turn. Utter politeness is the only treatment to give to *every* customer, regardless of attitude or size of purchase. If things get too hectic, try to call in help, explaining to waiting customers, "I think we need someone to help me help you."

Provide one more service by packing in the right order of fragility, with extra bags or a box to be sure the produce will get home unharmed. Warn the customer of anything that needs extra care or quick refrigeration.

Keep selling. Mention as a reminder (not a blunt hint) any tie-ins that may be useful if it seems the customer might have missed them. And keep in mind the slow-moving items that you may be able to bring up unobtrusively as your sales conversation goes forward. Help the customer's train of thought along—encourage the impulsive choice—yet without ever letting anyone feel you're pushing. Give extra suggestions to regular customers who may be only too happy to accept such extra service, but be wary about doing the same for strangers.

A little extra produce packed along with the purchased amount—the "farmer's dozen"—will be remembered after the food has been consumed. "Take one of these along to see if you'll want some next time you visit us." Or, "Have a couple of these for the children. A little surprise never spoiled anyone."

"See you soon." Finally, wish the customer (by name if possible) a happy day and come again soon. But beware of trite formulas, like "Have a nice day" or "Have a nice weekend." These can get awfully boring if you're greeted with them everywhere you shop. Try to vary the words from one customer to the next—anything that makes the customer think he's getting even a little individual treatment.

Your leavetaking with each customer can make a vital last impression. Squeezing out a hurried "Thank you very much" and turning instantly to the next in line or to the task you were taking care of is not likely to make a friend, no matter how busy the market is. Maybe most of the things you say to the many customers seem repetitive, dull from the thousands of times you've said them. But a customer hears them only once with each visit. Extras you put into a sale might never have occurred to them and may be just what it takes to convert a passerby to a productive repeat customer. Afraid you've said the same thing to a customer twice in successive visits? Forget it. As long as you say your piece sincerely, with every helpful intention, nobody will mind.

Chapter 6

The Root of Business

Anyone allergic to numbers (as I am) might quiver about the heart of the roadside business, which is keeping watch over the market's financial soundness. And though this has to be part of your everyday affairs, it isn't as scary as it looks, taking mostly attentiveness and some arithmetic. You're bringing in *money* all the time, and spending it too. But have you a system to *control* how it comes in and goes out? And what gets done with it while you have it, so that you can keep it longer and make it more productive?

Of course there's a way—and certainly it takes a little time and work—but to get your market to qualify as a business you must keep *records*. Record every penny, whatever it is for, and do it in a businesslike way—not just in a cash book or on register tape, but on organized sheets that tell you at any time just where the business stands. It's fine to say: "My brain's no sieve—I know where every cent is without piles of records." But then comes the day when you run into a shortage of cash, and you flounder about unable to remember a large expenditure.

HOW ARE WE DOING?

Record-keeping is like holding a stethoscope to the heart of your business. It's the only way to know at all times what the business *is* doing, and of knowing what to do and when something *needs* doing to keep the business sturdy. It helps you keep enough cash on hand to take advantage of a rare bargain or add a promising product to your line *when the moment comes for making the decision*. It's your way of knowing what it costs to operate the market.

When these operating costs are on paper, you can compare them with your current sales to get full control over operations. Once you're in business for a while you can also use your records to plot the market's past and its future. Knowing costs and incomes, you can put together financial goals, because you can see how the market is performing, how it was performing a month or a year ago and how it may act in months and years ahead.

Bookkeeping. The record-keeping system called bookkeeping always used to sound formidable, but then I learned that it's not just indispensable and must be done regularly and correctly, but that it really isn't hard. It's not much more challenging than balancing a checkbook. Of course, it's always nice to have someone in the family who *likes* to do the bookkeeping, if you prefer to put all your time into producing or managing.

Operating a business, even the smallest and simplest, calls on you to manage physical things as well as money. The market building, those who work in it, and the produce you sell, are your physical responsibilities. For managing both money and these less theoretical matters, you make decisions every day. No decision on money matters is possible without knowing the *then, now,* and *later.* Only records can tell you about these things. Detailed records can give most of the answers, but more important still they can bring up questions that might not occur to you if you didn't keep and analyze the records.

What *are* those questions? How is the business doing? Are volume *and* profits up over last month, last quarter, or last year? Is volume holding well now but supply threatening to shrink, to be followed by dropping profits (because of a long dry spell or wet spell)? The cause behind a shrinkage in profits usually shows up plainly in the records. Are your prices too high, cutting volume even though money seems to be coming in? Are your operating costs eating into the profits? Are you trying to carry too much of some products and ending up with low-profit leftovers or unsalable spoilage? Are you carrying too few products to make the volume you need? Is your markup too low? Are you carrying too many items, losing on slow movers so that the good sellers can't make up the difference? Are some of your sales down, though you hadn't noticed it (possibly because of competition or failing quality or unproductive salespeople)?

Finding problems. Some of these problems may be so obvious that you won't have to look beneath the financial surface to spot them. To find others in time to do something about them, you may have to really dig into the records to (1) identify the problems in the first place and (2) see the way to fix them. What is causing leaking profits or overweight costs? Which products bring in the best profits and which are the losers that should be dropped (because of high production or selling costs and small return)? Is one part of your business more profitable than others? Can you put more work and money into that part for greater profits still, cutting back on the less rewarding parts?

You are in business to make a living for yourself and family, and records will help you keep doing that and perhaps boost you into ways of doing it better. All questions and answers are there in the records if you keep them responsibly.

Taking time. No one can afford to spend half of each day keeping records and interpreting them instead of selling and managing—not to mention producing the food to sell. Still, you will have to sacrifice some hours to this chore. One or more of the seven major kinds of records mentioned here ought to cover the monetary goings-on in your market. Set up these "systems" before you start the business and review

them before each season begins. If you know in advance just
what your system will be and can start following it right
away, it will be second nature by the time you get busily
involved in everyday duties. Probably the biggest danger is
being so tied up at busy times that you neglect the records.

WHAT KIND OF RECORDS?

The one indispensable recordkeeping tool is the daily
accounting of sales and expenses—everything that comes in
or goes out. If you have employees (the family counts too),
you'll need a record of the time they put in and the wages they
earn. Then you should keep a record of sales by groups of
products, so that you can keep track of which are selling well
and which are duds.

We'll go deeper into the most useful kind of record—the
profit and loss statement—because it is the most revealing.
Inventory records are indispensable for knowing how much
of anything you had, have now, and may need at any time
during the season. The *balance sheet* gives you an overall
look at how things are going. Finally, *spoilage records* tell
accurately about overstocked produce so that you can cut
waste in the future. If any of these isn't explained clearly or
extensively enough here, one of your local competitors might
willingly help, or your county agent can direct you to
literature telling you how. An accountant is a good source
(for guidance on which records you will need, and for
samples tailored to your business).

RECORDS FOR LITTLE MARKETS

A cashbook. For the smallest market the least
complicated bookkeeping method is a cashbook. All you do is
post (list) all money you take in on one side of the book, and

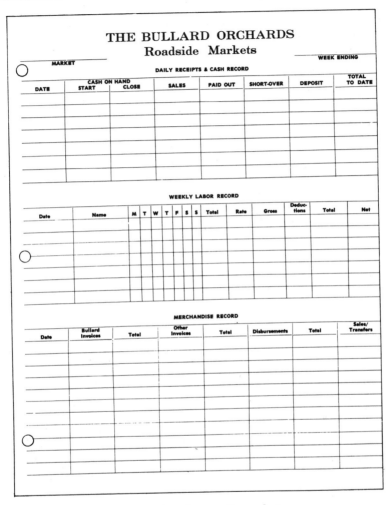

THE BULLARD ORCHARDS
Roadside Markets

MARKET _____ WEEK ENDING _____

DAILY RECEIPTS & CASH RECORD

DATE	CASH ON HAND START	CLOSE	SALES	PAID OUT	SHORT-OVER	DEPOSIT	TOTAL TO DATE

WEEKLY LABOR RECORD

Date	Name	M	T	W	T	F	S	S	Total	Rate	Gross	Deductions	Total	Net

MERCHANDISE RECORD

Date	Bullard Invoices	Total	Other Invoices	Total	Disbursements	Total	Sales/Transfers

A sample day book page for the small market.

enter everything you pay out on the other. The difference between the two tells how much cash you have on hand.

The smallest kind of operation also can handle its cash by the checkbook method. At the end of each day you prepare all the daily receipts for deposit in the bank—in a separate checking account just for the business. Then you can sit down and make all payments by check, logging in all deposits and checks with extreme care. With a big volume of sales, though, things can get out of hand because these methods are limited.

If you are working exclusively with a checking account one of the little shirt-pocket electronic calculators is handy. (One kind is set up for monitoring a checking account, with appropriate symbols and a memory that keeps your balance ready for instant recall.) For very little, you can buy record-keeping books at a stationery supplier. Or you may be able to get samples at least from your county agricultural agent, the Farm Bureau, or a business organization. These are some of the tools you will use in your trade. Get to know all of them and pick the ones that can make an efficient money manager of you.

A cash register. For the market business that's bigger, a cash register is useful and efficient enough to justify the investment. It can do many things that a cashbook can't. It also saves writing out a sales slip longhand, gives the customer a receipt, and prepares for you a record of each purchase. It can do other kinds of recording too, but most important (if you turn it back to zero at the end of the day) it tots up on its adding machine each sale as you make it and, when the day is over, tells you the cash receipts for the day. It also helps check on the employees' accuracy and honesty.

Many marketers with more than one sales employee have a separate cash drawer or register key for each one using the register. Comparing the record with the cash contents makes it sure that the cash taken in will be right there for counting when the operator finishes a day's work. It can also give you a subtotal for each line of produce, such as fruits, vegetables, processed foods, or other categories you have set up. With these you can watch sales and inventory closely.

Once you start keeping the records you'll soon want to see how well you're doing. In fact, you'd better check very soon and often, if only to know for tax times. Uncle Sam and the state tax collector will be just as interested as you are in seeing that your records are complete and accurate. With just two reports you can keep track of everything.

I repeat advice that's been passed down for years—don't

be afraid of the little accounting that needs to be done. It could make the difference between a successful business and a merely break-even venture. I've heard of growing marketers who get hooked on the numbers game. Such people think this part of the business is as exciting as selling, but of course it can also be depressing if negative numbers turn up too often. But set yourself up a good warning system with records and reports, and you can plug leaking profits before you have to start worrying. The places to start analyzing for news of your progress are the *profit and loss statement* and the *balance sheet*—the really indispensable instruments that tell you how things stand. Whichever tools you use, divide each record-keeping year into thirteen equal periods of four weeks each.

THE PROFIT AND LOSS STATEMENT

The profit and loss statement tells you the most vital fact about your business—how much the market is making for you—or the opposite. It can be useful whether you make it out every week, once a month, every quarter, or even once a year. Probably you'll want to work it out fairly often, and here's a place you may need help when things get busy. If you're working all day in the fields or at the market, or both, a helpmate (if she or he has time) may enjoy doing this mental exercise, though of course it takes a while for either of you to get practiced at it. Starting out with a good-sized market, it may be wise to go to a professional accountant—at least until you can handle it yourself. And if the income keeps growing while the business shows healthy signs, you'd be wise to hire an accountant to keep watch over the financial end of the business. It doesn't cost as much as you might think, because each accountant has a number of accounts, some big and some small. The accounting firm that's been around for a long time may have a lot of overhead and high prices, but plenty of perfectly able accountants are working on their own, and may well be able to charge more reasonable fees. A specialist should take care of the records, whether it is someone in the family, an accountant in the neighborhood, or a trusted employee.

Making profit and loss work. When you sit yourself down to fill out a profit and loss sheet follow these steps:

1. You write in income from sales (see example). For most marketers, this is the dollar volume of sales to the public at retail prices, but you might also have income from selling produce to wholesalers or to other farm markets or to other retailers. If you gave money back to any of the purchasers as refunds for whatever purpose, subtract that amount. Take each of these figures from the corresponding page in your record book.

2. Then figure how much the merchandise you sold to produce the income listed under number 1 was worth. (a) What was the value of your inventory (at wholesale prices) when this accounting period began (week, month, quarter, or year)? (b) What was the wholesale value of all produce transferred from your own farm to the roadside business? How much did the market "pay" your producing operation? (c) What was the total (if any) you spent on merchandise you bought to resell? (d) Add items *a, b,* and *c.* (e) Subtract the inventory value at the end of the accounting period from item *d.*

3. Now, subtract the value of all that you sold from the income the market earned from those sales, and you have a figure for your *gross* profit.

4. Next, list *all* your other expenses for this accounting period and total them.

5. Subtract the total of these expenses from the gross profit. The figure you get is your *net profit.*

6. If you are paying interest on a mortgage or other loans, deduct that total from the net profit. This final figure is your *taxable net profit.*

Spending. To find the expenses that will be listed under item 4, above, examine your expense records for everything you spent on labor (wages, commissions, overtime); taxes (federal, state, local, real estate, income, sales, excise, and any others); utilities (heating fuel, electricity, water,

---

MODEL FARM MARKET

Profit and Loss Statement for 197＿

January 1 to December 31, 197＿

INCOME

Retail Sales At Market	$37,606.26	92.1%
Wholesale Sales from Market	+3,217.60	7.9%
(to other markets)		
Total Gross Sales	$40,823.86	100.0%
Less Refunds and Allowances	- 44.50	.1%
Total Net Sales	$40,779.36	99.9%

COST OF MERCHANDISE SOLD

Wholesale Value of Produce Grown for Market	23,642.70	57.9%
Wholesale Purchases From Others	+1,151.05	2.8%
Total Cost of Merchandise Sold	-24,793.75	60.7%

GROSS PROFIT ON MARKET OPERATIONS | $15,985.61 | 39.2%

EXPENSES

Labor Hired	$2,338.20	5.7%
Salary Allowance for Family	6,000.00	14.7%
Supplies	1,090.65	2.7%
Building Depreciation	1,160.00	2.8%
Equipment Depreciation	278.45	.7%
Utilities	302.17	.7%
Maintenance	119.94	.3%
Advertising	228.30	.6%
Insurance	55.00	.1%
Taxes, Licenses & Fees	585.00	1.4%
Other	34.72	.1%
Total Expenses	-12,192.43	29.9%

NET PROFIT ON MARKET OPERATIONS	3,793.18	9.3%
Interest Cost (mortgage & loans)	- 640.00	1.6%
NET PROFIT BEFORE INCOME TAXES	$3,153.18	7.7%

telephone); advertising (all kinds); and packaging (bags, boxes, baskets). Experience will add items to this list, but it may also make you watch expenses for excesses and income for possible additions. Keeping track of cash as it flows in and out, and being aware of all the ways of managing money so that it will bring in most business at lowest cost—*that* is money management.

THE BALANCE SHEET

The balance sheet is not much more complicated than the profit and loss statement, but it is even more important. It shows at a glance how healthy the business is on the day you fill it out. Your banker can be a great help in setting up these forms, and, if they don't come out right, in finding out why. They may do just that, especially until you build some experience. Of course a banker will be more eager to help if you keep all or most of your banking business in his institution. Healthy accounts supported by active businesses make happy, helpful bankers.

The balance sheet sets out for your quick review (and your banker's) a detailed breakdown of the business's *assets, liabilities,* and *equity.* Its big purpose is to help you see if the financial condition of the business is turning upward or downward, or is holding on course. It saves you from having to go over all other records (daily, weekly, monthly, quarterly, or annual) to dig up that information. Of course, the sheet tells only what the business looks like on the day you fill it out. And that's another plus for balance sheets—you can spot trends in the market's financial life by looking at balance sheets from earlier accounting periods. It may be best to fill out a sheet regularly—every time you prepare an income statement.

Rain's coming—profits going. A trick that may be familiar to most marketers is to enter in each balance sheet a short account of what the weather was like during the period. A brief note may explain a day's fluctuating business or a lull lasting half a season. A normally rainy day or very high temperature can cut volume by a third, even when you

MODEL FARM MARKET

Balance Sheet

December 31, 19____

ASSETS

CURRENT ASSETS

Cash	$78.20	
Bank	800.67	
Accounts Receivable	62.00	
Total Current Assets		$940.87

FIXED ASSETS

Land (market site)	2,000.00	
Building (less depreciation)	12,461.88	
Equipment (less depreciation)	1,406.16	
Total Fixed Assets		15,868.04

TOTAL CURRENT AND FIXED ASSETS $16,808.91

LIABILITIES AND OWNER'S EQUITY

CURRENT LIABILITIES

Wages Payable	40.00	
Accounts Payable	128.44	
Notes Payable (equipment)	346.50	
Total Current Liabilities		514.94

FIXED LIABILITIES

Building Mortgage Payable	9,850.00	
Total Fixed Liabilities		9,850.00

TOTAL CURRENT AND FIXED LIABILITIES 10,364.94

OWNER'S EQUITY

Equity on January 1, 1965	4,433.47	
Net Profit for 1965 (after taxes)	2,010.50	
Total Owner's Equity		6,443.97

TOTAL LIABILITIES AND OWNER'S EQUITY $16,808.91

usually would have people crawling all over you for the new harvest. And watch the recovery after that bad day—you probably won't make back much more than 10 percent extra next day to balance the loss.

Make money count. In each accounting period, look closely at the really vital entries in the balance sheet. One thing this look will tell you is whether or not you are using your capital in the most efficient way. Cash on hand is part of this truth. Never have more cash than you need for the daily transactions that keep the business going. If you find any excess cash there, put it at once where it will do some good. Pay debts with it to cut down on high-interest loans. Invest the money in assets that will earn interest for you, or in other sound investments. Or plow it into land (which can be the most productive investment by far), or building, or equipment.

Credit? When you're getting a market started, expect requests for credit from your customers, both friends and strangers. Regular customers, either individuals or businesses, will ask you to do them this service, a perfectly legitimate, customary practice. But unless you're prepared to set up a full-fledged *accounts receivable* operation and pay for it with your time or your accountant's fee, make it clear to those who ask you to put it on the bill that you're simply not in a position to handle credit. Then make no exceptions till the day when you are ready to tie up your money for other people's convenience and are able to do without the immediate cash payments that most marketers depend on. When you do extend credit, set a definite period for payment and follow up carefully, collecting the full amount each customer owes before you allow more charging. There's much to be said for being free with credit, because it can encourage larger purchases. Sometimes though, it attracts the kind of customers who live by credit. Credit does make paper work and expense, and some people don't like to be collected from.

On the other side of the ledger, anyone *you* go to for credit, especially than banker friend, will ask questions that probe your business's financial soundness. Lenders will look for answers to the following questions on your balance sheet:

(1) How do current assets compare with current liabilities?

(2) How do your current liabilities look when you set them alongside the market's current net worth?

(3) What percentage of return are you getting on your investments, and what is your total return?

(4) How high a return are you getting on your tangible net worth (your equity)?

(5) How is the turnover on your working capital running?

FORMS TO RUN YOUR
BUSINESS BY

The forms we show here, though just a handful chosen from the armload of possibilities, may be all you'll need. Instead of going into detail explaining their uses, as I did for the profit and loss statement, I'll leave these to your inventiveness. Wherever the forms seem less than clear in explaining themselves, ask for a short lesson from your extension agent. He may have forms that are better suited to your market, because they are simpler or more complex, depending on your home-grown problems. Play around with the forms, and let experience decide which you are likely to tend most carefully and regularly. Unsuitable forms often are more and more ignored and for that reason can hurt the market badly.

CAPITAL QUESTIONS

As I mentioned earlier, it becomes costly in taxes and (R. Alden Miller at the University of Massachusetts says it more strongly), it is unbusinesslike not to set your accounting system up so that the market pays the farm for everything you produce and sell. That's a good way of making sure you are using the right markup. Certainly, your farm-grown produce is worth at least as much as the wholesale price; it is also supposed to be better than foods people buy in the wholesale marketplace. You'll need a simple way of keeping track of the transactions, though, and Mr. Miller tells of one producer-retailer who bought a bunch of duplicate receipt pads at the dime store. For each item delivered to the stand from the farm, he made out a ticket with one copy for the stand and the other for the farm. Whoever hauled the produce from the farm to the market's preparation room filled out the duplicate ticket with the going wholesale price. That price can be taken from a reference sheet you can put together quickly from the prices listed by the nearest wholesale produce market. The Boston market, for instance, publishes the seasonal average for all the native-grown commodities.

Short of cash? Handling cash is a special challenge for the roadside marketer. Roger G. Ginder says that the secret here lies in knowing how much cash is enough. The way he sees the problem, it begins with the extremely seasonal quality in growing and selling produce (unless, of course, you diversify to spread your season out). For many marketers, cash flows in rapidly during the growing and harvesting season. That's all to the good, if you know what to do with it.

The trouble comes when your off-season rolls around. Even shutting down the market completely doesn't stop money from draining out for everyday family expenses, repairing and expanding and between-seasons advertising. Where you had a surplus of cash during the busy season, you are suddenly faced with a cash outflow when business is quiet. Manage surplus cash that was gathered in along with the harvests by investing it shrewdly, and your only problem is running short of operating cash when things get busy again next season. That could be ruinously expensive, not just because you might miss a bargain, but cash might be pinched enough to make you cut back on profitable lines that you depend on most. A simple solution is not to be caught with your operating capital down.

Make more with money. Here's how Ginder suggests handling surplus cash when you have it, so that you will neither lose revenue from it nor get caught short:

(1) Find out exactly how much you have; be conservative and you won't overestimate the amount.

(2) Figure how much cash you will need in the coming months and how much (if any) you can set aside to earn money in other ways—some that you don't need to use directly in the business.

For the investable money, you may want to pick short-term investments suggested by your friendly banker, or savings accounts if you, your accountant, and the banker think that's the best place. The certificates of deposit that earn more interest than savings accounts, and sometimes more than most other forms of investment, may be too restrictive, tying up money that should be reachable in a hurry. Certificates can be costly, too, if you are forced to cash them in early. The checking account usually works only by providing the cash you need every day of the season for operating the market. Unless your bank has one of the checking accounts that pays interest (but watch the hidden costs), the only one who will earn money is the banker.

Other ways of avoiding shortness of cash are somewhat obvious, like (1) be rich, and (2) prepare a budget for the whole selling season. Your records will tell when cash is likely to pour in and if it might run short at any time. If you happen not to be blessed with surplus cash right now, but you can foresee a time when a little extra might be indispensable, try to arrange now for credit, before the need comes. Quick decisions and undelayed loans can make the difference between a comfortable profit and no profit at all. Even worse, bills coming in when cash is short can hurt a hard-earned reputation for quick and reliable bill-paying. A damaged credit rating can last a long time, no matter what caused the damage and how soon you recovered.

Earn by thrift. Managing money so that it will grow doesn't necessarily demand that you grow more produce, add new lines of produce, or even sell more by superb salesmanship of everything you now grow, says Roger Ginder. You can do even better by finding ways of cutting costs.

Most people think that to get higher profits they must get more money moving into the cash register. But think about it a little. Cut your costs by a dollar and your profits (before taxes) will give you a full dollar's worth. To gain a dollar by increasing sales, you've got to make several dollars for that one, because of overhead expenses. And when you believe you're already getting the best out of your selling, it can take a very hard effort to make the extra show on your profit and loss sheet—perhaps so hard that you'll spoil your market's reputation as a noncommercial, friendly operation.

Let's look, then, at Mr. Ginder's explanation of how this method works. Say that you use a 50 percent markup to cover all your overhead costs, and your overall profit margin (which is *not* the same as markup) is 20 percent of the total sales figure. If you want to increase your clear profit by $1,000, you'll have to expand sales by $5,000. But then let's say that by analyzing your operations you find $1,000 in costs that you can eliminate. That $1,000 then becomes clear profit (before taxes), unless you've shaved costs too closely somewhere (so much that the tightness will be reflected in decreased sales). For every dollar you'd add to profits by selling more, you'll have to sell $5 more in produce. The dollar you save on costs is worth $5 in sales, and so will bring in $1,000 with no extra sales effort, which is the same as adding $5,000 in sales.

Of course if your margin is higher than 50 percent, a smaller increase in sales will up the profit each dollar brings in. But then your margin can't go ballooning too far without causing higher prices—which could mean smaller sales. Going at it the other way around: if your profit margin is lower, you'll need more volume for each dollar of profit. From all this circular-sounding reasoning, you can see that any saving in costs brings more income at lower profit margins. Be awake every minute for ways of cutting costs *that won't hurt sales.* (See Roger Ginder's table and drawing that brings it all to life.)

EFFECTS OF SALES INCREASES AND
COST SAVINGS ON PROFIT UNDER
DIFFERENT PRE-TAX PROFIT MARGINS

With a pre-tax profit margin of

A cost savings of	33% on sales equals a sales increase of	25% on sales equals a sales increase of	20% on sales equals a sales increase of	16% on sales equals a sales increase of	12% on sales equals a sales increase of	10% on sales equals a sales increase of
$ 250	$ 750	$1,000	$1,250	$1,500	$ 2,000	$ 2,500
$ 500	$1,500	$2,000	$2,500	$3,000	$ 4,000	$ 5,000
$ 750	$2,100	$3,000	$3,700	$4,500	$ 6,000	$ 7,500
$1,000	$3,000	$4,000	$5,000	$6,000	$ 8,000	$10,000
$1,500	$4,500	$6,000	$7,500	$9,000	$12,000	$15,000

* Roger G. Ginder, in *Roadside Market News,* June, 1971.

Keep a tight rein. These suggestions for lowering costs may look like the common sense each of us was born with, but as Roger Ginder says, they also come from good business sense groomed by years of experience. Don't slice meat instead of fat from your operation; cut the waste caused by spoilage and damage. Buy and handle produce as if it were delicate as the bloom on the grape—it is. Look for discounts you can take advantage of, sometimes by buying in quantity, by paying cash, or by making purchases of equipment and supplies outside the regular season. Watch your pennies when you buy supplies—don't skin a flea for a cent, but conserve as much as you can in your spending. Cut waste in any part of your operation: time, materials, effort. Consider recycling discarded vegetable matter by composting it, a good way of saving on fertilizer. Use your best ability in money management, putting every bit of capital you spend through a multiple test, digging for alternative uses you could put the money to, perhaps finding ways that would make greater profits. Spend only on the most profitable items. For expensive equipment that isn't constantly used, renting or leasing may be far better than buying it, if you can plan just when you will need the equipment. Subject everything that goes into the market to your management sense (common sense that's gone to school). Using things a little differently may mean doing things more efficiently, saving money with every short cut.

Raise volume. Cutting costs, then, is a quick way of upping profits, though it's neither riskless nor easy. But increasing volume can do the same thing, and is usually a sign that the business is healthy. Staking everything on bigger volume may make a success of you. But combining efficiency and growth is the best way to manage.

TAXES

One expense that requires really tight management is taxes. In roadside marketing you've chosen a business that gives you an automatic tax advantage. Like other businesses (including production) that depend on the land and the atmosphere above it, income from marketing fluctuates from one year to the next. If you judge that your income will be higher than in other years, because of high wholesale prices (which means you can charge a higher markup), or because of more efficient production, you can level off the excess and reduce taxable income. Buy as many supplies before December 31 as you foresee a need for (equipment, baskets, bags, paint), and pay for them before that date to make the expense deductible from your taxes for that year. Make investments in the building or in heavy equipment; expand the market; add capacity to your cooler; buy a new truck or trailer. And save money on these by buying the current year's model instead of waiting for the not very different next year's model. Though you may lose something when it's time to replace the equipment, a gain is possible by picking up a leftover or overstocked model. In figuring your taxes, charge to the market only the portions of the time that double-duty items, like cars and trucks, are used for the market.

Depreciate early. Another method for writing off excess profits without losing heavily is to choose rapid depreciation schedules on your more lasting investments, weighting the depreciation toward the earlier years in the asset's life and taking some of the financial burden off its later years. Your banker or Internal Revenue Service office can be of great help in choosing these methods or suggesting others.

Depreciate late. But what if this year's profits look grimmer than usual and *next* year's seem promising? Then put off expensive purchases for a year. Arrange, if you can, to pay after the first of the year for some of the items you will need—if interest rates on borrowed money won't chew up the money you will save. Put off buying some of the things that will depreciate over a longer time. If you really need those now, cut the pain by spreading the depreciation over future years when prosperity may come again. The IRS office could come up with unsuspected ideas to help you out of a momentary shortage.

EXPECT THE WORST—INSURE

Another part of money management has to do with shrinking the risk that disaster will ruin your property until it is low enough to be bearable, that is, affordable. It's called insurance, and I thank Roger Ginder again for his suggestions on how to gauge your need for it. The way the economy is going, the costs for replacing property that you lose to fire, theft, and vandalism are climbing quicker than the crime rate. And accident claims, swollen by liberal judgments, are wiping out formerly adequate coverage. To figure out which risks are most threatening to you and what kinds of coverage you may need and can pay for, you'll need the insurance agent's help. The things to consider are your market's special characteristics, your financial position—secure, solvent, barely adequate, or broke—and just how much risk your finances will let you take without sinking you into a dangerous position. Your fire insurance policy should reflect the current value of your assets—*replacement* cost, not your depreciated cost. Liability insurance on the high side costs little more than minimal coverage. Take full safety precautions and the premiums may be reasonable anyway. Make sure everything is covered—grounds, buildings and equipment, not to mention employees and customers.

Once every year—or more than that when big changes come—review all your coverages with your agent, trimming unwanted items and adding to the umbrella anything new that needs protection. Figure out where you are, what you have, and how much you can afford to lose. Getting all your insurance from one broker, including life and automobile coverage, is a convenience for both of you, may make it easier to get claims paid off, and could bring the cost down. Choosing the broker is best done, like so many other things, by listening to word-of-mouth among friendly local marketers. Some companies can give you a much better deal in premiums or service or in settling claims. Everyone tells us to shop around for insurance as we do for cars, and for once everyone is right. One company in your area may be much better.

Read up on protection. Because inadequate coverage can be a fatal weakness in your management, I think having extra facts can do nothing but good. Much of the material you'll read here comes from a condensation Ransom A. Blakeley made of a Small Business Administration booklet (Management Series No. 30, SBA, Washington 25, D.C., 1963). You can get the condensed version by writing to Purdue University or the full booklet from Superintendent of

Documents, United States Government Printing Office, Washington 20402. I hope it will be kept up to date.

Insurance is a necessary luxury because it lets you trade a large but uncertain loss that you haven't suffered yet for a small but certain loss now, which is called the *premium.* Trading certainty for uncertainty or reducing your risks is the service insurance companies sell. Once you have the insurance, it can also cut your worries about disaster hanging over the market, free you to undertake new and bigger operations, release for investment funds that you might otherwise feel you had to set aside to cover losses yourself, prevent losses by making you think about them and do something before they come. It can also ease your way to credit.

Don't overprotect. You don't want to insure yourself against trivial losses, obviously—risks that wouldn't hurt and that you can absorb easily from operating capital, the money you cover the market's everyday expenses with. Someone long in the business with a big market could think $10,000 loss trivial. Most small markets, though, would suffer at losing $1,000 or less. For a loss that could be major, outside help is called for, and that means the insurance companies.

Unnecessary coverage is anything you could afford to lose or would not bother to replace; it is also anything that is worth less than the premiums you'd pay to cover it. You can see that kind of coverage most easily in car insurance. For anything like a dilapidated shed or barn that is in such bad shape you probably wouldn't rebuild it if it did burn, save money by not getting it covered—but ask your agent if that's acceptable. As with other ways of saving on insurance, you may have to make it very clear to the agent that you want to leave something uncovered, or you'll find too late that you've been paying for something that wasn't worth it. With a business big enough to need more than one or two motorized vehicles, you might also qualify for less expensive "fleet" insurance.

The small market, and even the medium-sized one, can't possibly be covered at a reasonable cost for every disaster.

But be sure not to fall into the wrong kind of thinking about insurance: "Fire insurance is so expensive that I can't pay for it; besides, I don't want to tie up all that money in premiums. It's money that never comes back." If that were true, you'd have a tough time replacing the market if you lost it, and starting all over again would be the next move. It's the really big risks (like a total loss) that insurance is meant to save you from. And the premiums, though they're never cheap, can be gotten down to where they don't eat up all your cash.

Cut losses and premiums. The name that insurance companies give to one way of cutting premiums and keeping property safe is *prevention of loss.* Do everything possible to remove risks; to protect against burglary; and to make sure your buildings and grounds are safe for the public and yourself, free of accidents and hazards to health. You can think of many such risk-reducers, and many more can be learned from fire and police departments and insurance agents. They are as interested as you in keeping your market safe and whole. The insurance people especially want to help (the ones who know their jobs), because they would just as soon collect premiums from all of us forever and never have to pay a claim. It's beneficial, too, to lower the risks. It can reduce premiums to more painless amounts. And that lowers *your* cost of doing business.

Transferring risks is an alternative to buying insurance, though it isn't practical or available for most people. When you lease cars, trucks, and large equipment, the company doing the leasing usually pays the premiums, not you—except that the cost, of course, is part of the rental fee.

LIABILITY INSURANCE

Liability insurance must be covered in your plan. The common law and the statutory law both require you to make sure you are not negligent toward customers, employees, and anyone you do business with. *Negligence* here means *your failure to exercise the care required under the circumstances,* which sounds like, and is, a fuzzy legal notion. Fuzzy or not, it can cost you everything if you are found negligent. A simple thing like a customer falling on your slippery, just-washed floor can make you liable to a claim for damages, even though you cautiously post signs warning of the danger. You're expected to maintain a place safe for customers to come into. You cannot defend yourself by saying you failed to exercise due care unintentionally; how could you know that those huge platform shoes weren't safe on soapy surfaces? Doesn't matter. You're at fault, not those who push dangerous footgear on the gullible public. Most accidents are, after all, wholly unintentional. But generally in accidents on business premises arising out of business operations, the courts strongly presume that negligence (yours) caused the accident.

What kind and how much? One of the worst errors when insuring a small business is not to carry the right kind and amount of liability insurance, the kind that covers you if you are found liable for an injury to a stranger (or to a friend for that matter). You need it both on vehicles and on the market, of course. No one can think of depending on an accident victim's good will or on one's powers of persuasion to get off for a small sum if anything did happen. Unhappily, people do hurt themselves on other people's property as well as their own. And one judgment against you for one accident could wipe out all your business assets—even force you to liquidate the business to pay the damages.

The courts are severe in protecting the public against negligence committed in places of business, intentionally or not. They consistently broaden the idea of legal liability and award bigger and still bigger amounts to injured people. They are also known to award huge sums for such "damages" as mental anguish resulting from an accident. And they continue to weaken defenses that used to be acceptable in negligence cases. These trends in the courts prove only that you need extra-thorough coverage in liability insurance with a reputable company and agency.

What are you paying for? The liability policy you want probably will cover several kinds of losses:

(1) *liability judgments* which you become legally obligated to pay because someone suffers bodily injury or damage to property—which you cause accidentally,

(2) *expenses* you incur for immediate medical and surgical relief at the time the accident happens,

(3) *costs of defending against suits* for bodily injury or property damage, even if the suit has no real basis,

(4) *your own expenses* in the investigation, defense, or settlement of an accident claim against you,

(5) *cost of court bonds* or interest on judgments that mount up during an appeal.

With the one liability policy you can be covered for all the expense (if not all the trouble) of settling a liability suit. In fact, just having an insurer who will handle the "nuisance suit," the trouble that forever plagues all businessmen, is in itself worth the cost of the protection.

Insurance companies may figure the rates you must pay by the amount of floor area in your market, your front footage on a highway, or your sales volume. Where your market is and what limits of liability you choose will affect the premium you'll pay. Do not restrict these limits too tightly. As you've probably learned in buying car insurance, high coverage costs very little more than the lowest you can get, and it can be worth a great deal more when trouble comes.

Workers' Protection

Starting out with a sizable market (or growing into one) usually means having outside help. You have to get to know about workmen's compensation and employer liability insurance. The common law and the Occupational Safety and Health Act require that you as an employer (1) provide your employees a safe place to work, (2) hire competent fellow employees, (3) provide safe tools, and (4) warn your employees of any danger. Under both common law and workmen's compensation laws you are liable for damage claims an employee may bring against you if you fail to live up to any of these duties. Be sure to read your workmen's compensation rules thoroughly before you hire anyone. If the business is small and you have few employees (no more than four in some states), you may not have to get this coverage. But then you must pay all the expenses if an employee is hurt and sues you.

Your defenses. Three defenses are possible if an employee sues, assuming you are in the right as far as you know:

(1) Any employee assumes some risks immediately upon accepting a job.

(2) Admitted or not, the employee may be wholly or partly to blame for the accident (this is called *contributory* negligence).

(3) The accident may have been caused by a fellow employee and not by your negligence.

Many things may cause an accident, and the harm may be tiny or fatal. These defenses are not enough, when you consider all the reasons an employee may have for suing, but getting rid of hazards and covering yourself against unforeseen and potentially destructive legal expenses is no more than the sensible thing to do. Remember, before the law *you* are liable, even though you didn't directly cause an accident. Prevention and insurance coverage are your best defenses—really your only ones—and they cost very little compared with how much they might save you. True, many people suffer the illness of being insurance-poor, but they are far better off expensively covered than exposed and broke.

PLAN YOUR PROTECTION

Ransom Blakeley summarizes the important steps in planning your coverage:

(1) Decide which method of covering the risks is best financially.

(2) Cover your biggest risk first and the less severe ones later when your income grows.

(3) Use the deductibles (you pay the first $50 or $100) to get adequate coverage at lowest cost.

(4) Review your coverage regularly (once a year anyway) instead of simply renewing the policies when they come due. Your agent usually won't need asking when the time comes, because repeat business is healthy for him, too, but you should be ready before he is with questions and a plan for the coming year.

(5) Check with other marketers before buying *and* before renewing insurance coverage. One thing you can gain by comparing notes is whether or not the premiums you're paying are in line with those paid by other people who have similar coverage.

(6) The amount and quality of service you get from your insurance company may vary with the price you pay. Find out all you can about the agency's reputation for service, fairness and speed in paying claims.

(7) Cover the real risks—one of which is bonding employees who handle cash for you. You may not know till it's too late that someone you believed beyond suspicion has a hand in the till.

(8) Buy all your coverage from one company. That might cost a little more because you don't shop around for every policy, but it could just as well save you some (if your agent gives you a break for multiple policies), and assure you of consistently good service.

Chapter 7

Advertising: What, Why, and How

Roadside marketers you talk to may say that well-grown, freshly picked produce is an advertisement all by itself—all you have to do is set it out any old way and its own qualities will sell it for you.

Chances are that these confident people have been in business a long time and have built up a fine collection of regular customers. When you're all set in business it's not easy to think back on how tough it is just getting started. And if you're lucky enough to have a following (or to pick one up by inheriting or buying an established business), you may not need much advertising to do a comfortable amount of business. With a combination of production and selling that seems just right, why extend yourself to drag in crowds? Aren't the customers as happy with you as you are with them? If you advertise widely and successfully it will mean growing or buying more produce and spending even more time selling. Growth snowballs, or it seems that way, and it can end by turning you into a commercial operator, which may be just the thing you'd planned against. Or *is* that what you're working for?

For the newcomer by the roadside, even a small start calls for plans and action to get things moving. Word has to get out that a new market, well stocked with excellent foods at fair prices, is being opened by a marketer who's interested in serving people the best, and is ready and eager for their patronage. For the new marketer, advertising means making sure that enough people know he's there. It's no good working yourself ragged cultivating good produce and setting up a business that nobody comes near.

Advertising is a kind of education, teaching people that you have something they want. It can be done in many ways: spreading good will by word-of-mouth from friend to friend, paying to have your news printed in the newspaper, or announcing it by voice and pictures on radio or television. It also is displaying your goods for all to see, and it is promoting your service—that is, impressing one thought on as many people as are willing to pay attention: They *ought* to care about your service because it's for *them.*

PROMOTE YOUR PRODUCT

Promotion means showing dramatically what your product is and what it can do for people who buy it. All these are ways of selling—some at a distance and others in the market. The one sure thing about advertising and promotion in any form is that you've got to be perfectly straightforward in everything you say and do. Encouraging people to come and buy is what you do. But *how* you do it is the thing that will matter most over the years. Total honesty, absolutely factual talk and practices are the ways of getting and keeping the customers you need.

Simplest is best. The oldest and still the best way of advertising is the service that your pleased customers can do for you in return for the good things you offer them. This is word-of-mouth—pleased customers carrying news to other people, convincing them that your offerings are good for them too. It costs nothing but hard work and a friendly attitude. That is why agricultural advisors agree on one rule for direct marketing: *Once you have the best produce you can grow, greet the customers, whether they are buying or not, as*

Entice customers as this market does, with displays of produce and tools.

though they were friends you can help. Word-of-mouth, says M. R. Cravens, is the only guaranteed way of getting customers who will stick. And keeping those customers happy is just as productive. Yet even the marketers who depend almost wholly on this spreading of good will back it with other kinds of advertising in limited amounts.

It may seem a shame to compromise this way, which can be almost totally independent, by using the methods usually connected with the mass marketers, who spend on advertising as if they were selling *it* and not produce. Yet advertising is a little like the poison that can sustain life—even the most independent, self-reliant marketer needs it, especially when business needs a push to get started or to grow. As a part of business, advertising is almost indispensable to keep our consuming economy and your market going.

A heartening thought is that when you advertise you start with an advantage. The roadside marketing business has that special image in the public mind—as a hearty, down-to-earth endeavor. Stay noncommercial in every way you can, but *not* by giving up the benefits that sensible advertising can bring.

How to Go About It

How do you get a helpful campaign going—one that will bring in customers who then may become walking billboards for you?

Do it yourself. I don't think you need to run to an advertising agency unless you have or expect to have a business climbing quickly to the $25,000 or $50,000 level. Not that smaller businesses can't profit by getting a professional's services, but the fabled American elevator to the clouds, your own bootstrap, still gets people there, I hear. A lot of people would rather do it themselves than pay others to spread their news. The alternative, of course, is going directly to the medium that will carry your message to the people—go to the newspaper's or radio station's advertising representative. If you don't get all the help you need there, maybe you haven't gone to the right ones. Also, find out where your nearby competitors do their advertising. Then the problem you face is either finding a better place to handle your advertising business, or arranging to have the same source do a better job. Be very careful, though, not to copy anyone else's ads.

Start your campaign early. Even before you open the market for the first day of business, Lou Albano says, you can be preparing potential customers by spreading the word yourself, dropping in on local merchants and leaving them a printed card or sheet announcing your opening. Any organization you belong to can be fertile ground for cultivating good words about yourself and your venture. You can run a small announcement in your local paper, telling about the market, its produce, the opening date, and any background that may seem important, like how you got the idea of selling by the roadside. You could even build the first small advertisement into a series—publishing short, appealing notices that climax about a week before you open with the traditional news: a grand new entrance into business! A campaign like that can be inexpensive and is likely to do you far more good than one half-hearted ad stuck in the paper at the last minute before you open.

SIGN LANGUAGE

The first words many people will see about your enterprise may be your road signs, your outdoor advertising. Here you can make an effective start with an informal, restrained, tasteful sales appeal, at once setting you apart from the high-pressure stuff ad agencies seem to feel is the only way to get to the public's eyes and mind. The dayglo and neon skyscraper vulgarities that many restaurant and motel and other commercial people erect at great expense may be necessary for their kind of business, which sometimes has to depend heavily on transients. Maybe they have to hit the world over the head to get the message across. You don't. It's economically sensible to advertise on the approach signs, telling people as they near your market that you're there and they're welcome. All the signs need to be is visible, readable, attractive, and well cared for.

Planned appeal. Start planning your signs by finding out the local zoning regulations: how big a sign can be on your building or off it, what kind of support signs must have, how close to the road, how far from the ground, how many you're allowed and at what intervals. These regulations may seem tight, but they make it easier for you to do a job as effective as other advertisers without spending too much. Put signs far enough away from the market to give advance notice to drivers and still have the signs on your own land if you can. The teaser trick places signs a mile or more from the market for far-off attention getting, and others closer in, narrowing the distance marked on the signs from three miles to one, then 1,500 yards, 1,000 yards, and finally 500 feet. For these you'll probably have to approach the ones who own the land where the distant signs would be to get permission. In some areas such serial signs are outlawed.

Most people in open parts of the country still may not charge for space to put up a small, tasteful sign. You might have to pay a little in cash or produce for some of them. You'll cover the road in both directions from the market, choosing spots not occupied by other people's signs and not obscured by trees, brush, or grasses that grow too high. Try to get an understanding that no other signs will be put close to yours. This probably is prohibited by zoning laws anyway, and it clogs the open landscape (which is a big reason for coming to the country to buy), spoils the view, and cancels any effect each sign might have off by itself.

The average market sign is about 23 square feet in area, and the rectangular shape is most common and easiest to read. A sign painter, if you can find one, will put together the kind of impression you want to make on people, without making the job look too polished and commercial. Place signs around the market as carefully as on the road. They may be useful above the front, at either end on the structure itself or out by the road where passersby can spot your entrance from either direction. One hazard some people forget is hiding the market or its most appealing visual features—the produce or a scenic country setting—with too many signs.

Make your mark. Inventing a *logotype,* a symbol that will be recognizable and attention-getting, is a profitable plan. It can appear on all signs, in your displays, and in advertising matter in newspapers, on television and on printed containers. It has to be striking (not in size but in design and color), easy to see, to read, and to remember, and different from any that people may see nearby. The thing itself and its design count heavily. That device or trade mark isn't hard to come up with—start by thinking about the market's name (or your own if they're different), or your initials, or your most important product, or something about the building or its surroundings, or a phrase describing the market, its produce, or special services you offer.

What to show and say. Work up the signs along with eye-catching displays, combined near the market with something appropriate, like brightly colored farm equipment—a wagon still seems the most familiar symbol, piled high with the produce you specialize in. An oversized copy of a fruit or vegetable is too cute for some people, but try a bright barn, a white picket fence, lots of flowers, maybe a mill wheel or two, antique farm equipment—anything countrylike to get attention without gaudy artificial things. Cluttered displays or signs can make a damaging first impression. It's easy for people to keep moving if they can't see the market for the junky attention-getting devices.

Joseph F. Hauck mentions signs that tell what's in season, placed at or near the market. These are a service in themselves and have to be kept up to the minute so that regular customers will know when to stop for a seasonal specialty. When you write the signs, follow an advertising principle that applies to them even more than to printed ads—play up the strongest facts about your produce: *Freshly Picked,* or *Harvests Twice A Week,* or *Tree-Ripened Fruit,* or *Nothing But Native Vegetables,* or *We Sell Only Fruits We Grow,* or *All Fresh From Our Fields,* or *From Tree To Table,* or *All Organically Good.* These are exclusively *your* selling points. No supermarkets and few non-chain grocery stores can truthfully claim as much freshness and ripeness.

Readable colors. Pick the colors and styles of lettering to go on the signs for their visibility and readability, not to mention good looks. R. Alden Miller tells us that green letters on a white background are easiest to read. Red on white is supposed to stimulate sales, as you might well believe if you pay attention to the supermarketer's choices. Capital first letters and lower case words in a fairly large size (with the lower case almost as big as the capitals) are more quickly recognized than a whole line of capital letters.

Maintenance is a very important word in the sign business, too. Shabby signs inspire little confidence. Check every sign at least once a year for wearing and visibility—close up. Deterioration is hard to spot from a hundred yards out, or even twenty feet. Nailing a sign to a tree is the simplest way of getting it up, but the tree may be injured. A well-made, vandal-proof support standing clear of underbrush might let you put signs in otherwise inconvenient places. Eight or ten feet seems about the right height unless the signs are very close to the road, which means they can be a little lower. The higher you put them, though, the better you'll foil the plinkers and rock-throwers who welcome a neat new sign to demolish. Have the angle of the approach signs suit the direction the cars will be coming from, especially on a curve. A sign aimed at a right angle to the road or parallel to it may not give people time enough to spot and read it. Make the support as strong as you can afford to or as your ingenuity will allow; railroad ties make a good base that's no pushover for funloving vandals.

Get it right. Beware of misspellings. Check every word on your sign against a dictionary. It's more common than you'd think when a beautiful, effective sign is finished, to find that you or the sign painter put in one letter too many or too few, or flipped one upside down or backward. Don't advertise *Home Groan Vegetables.*

GET IT IN PRINT

Everyone has to have a few signs to mark the market, but what about the more competitive kinds of advertising? Is it wise or necessary to go to the trouble and expense of publishing ads? When do you have to go to a bigger public for more sales?

First thing to decide is whether the audience you'll be reaching to is big enough to make the investment worthwhile. You can choose *weekly newspapers* or the next step after the weeklies, the *daily* papers, which have bigger circulations but not necessarily more expensive rates per reader reached. Local *shoppers' guides* are good for door-to-door delivery and especially to reach summer people and other visitors. Some guides are put out too, by groups of merchants sharing the expense. *County or regional magazines* get to still wider audiences, including people normally too far away ever to hear of you or to travel to your market easily. *Handbills* or circulars sometimes are read by people who may be interested in visiting your market, even in buying something from you. *Printed packaging materials* have a different effect, carrying your name among the people who've bought from you already and spreading it to friends and neighbors, or even to passersby who happen to see the packages. These cost you little beyond the price of the materials. If you want to get more of a message than the market's name in the customer's hands, *bag inserts* can do it, also inexpensively, and they are likely to be read.

The local newspaper. A weekly especially will give you a small, relatively inexpensive start. Your ad, no matter how unpretentious, may be read by just about everyone in town who can read. Even buried in the classifieds, it will probably have a chance of being read or getting at least a passing glance.

After your series announcing the opening date, you may want to expand into a small ad outside the classified columns to announce upcoming harvest dates, like first corn of the season. If you can afford to keep ads running all season, people may come right out and tell you they first learned of the market from the ad in the paper. In a watershed of towns whose populations read several local papers, it may pay to put little ads in all of them.

Find out how well such an ad is likely to be spread around the communities that your customers might come from, and how much it will cost. Question the newspaper sales office about how many subscribers live within the circle that you think holds all the people in your trading area, say a radius of seven or eight miles, which is about the longest drive the average regular customer is willing to make for fresh produce. Say the newspaper's circulation hits a thousand homes in that trading area and the charge for a display ad is $50, then your cost for each house the ad reaches is just 5 cents. A classified ad will be cheaper than that, of course, carrying quite a few words for many weeks, if you feel the ad will draw enough eyes.

For a bigger display ad, it might be worth the extra effort and cost to change the message at least once a month or more often, which you should do anyway as new crops ripen. You or one of your helpers should be prepared to handle this important job—running the market's advertising—

regularly. Always check the paper to see that the ad is there, without misleading errors or badly broken type.

A daily paper. Daily papers give relatively inexpensive advertising if you decide to saturate your marketing area with a heavier barrage or want to reach out to a broader area, maybe to include a bigger nearby town or city. But go for regular customers first, not the unreliable droppers-in who could far outnumber the few regulars you might gain by distant advertising. And in evaluating all the newspapers that reach your target area, consider the advantages and disadvantages. Try to blanket the right socio-economic groups, usually the middle-class, fairly comfortably off people. You might tie into your advertising campaign some novelties that will spread the word farther still: even balloons, pencils, calendars or matchbooks.

MEDIA ADVERTISING

Let's review some of the steps in commercial advertising before going on to other parts of the business. First, when do you use commercial advertising? For the new business, as I've mentioned, getting the word spread around may be an indispensable first move.

For the established marketer who needs to build business or simply *wants* to, the media pave the way to growth. You just can't become known to enough of the people who buy fresh produce to keep you going or growing, unless you get your story before several times as many eyes and ears.

When? You'll want to advertise at the times when the response is going to be biggest and most profitable: a grand opening, startup day of a new season, important harvest days, special sale dates, any times of bounty or surplus, and peak trading days of the week, month, and season. Keep your mind and budget ready for these times. Then, backed by your daily records and statements, you'll know when an advertising shot in the arm is called for.

Budgeting ads. How much is enough to spend for advertising? At first, 2 or 3 per cent of your annual gross sales should cover the cost of all the advertising you need. It may be enough to continue with, as well.

Find out from the sales manager how the newspaper or radio station charges for each ad, having decided in advance what kind of ad you want, how much time or space you must prepare copy for, what kind of copy they need. Get data on their readership or listening audience, broken down by area. Learn what other businesses like yours they handle.

Assessing it. Measure how effective your advertising is, but not by how much you have spent or by the results promised. It's hard to tell just how many people come to you strictly because of your ads, but after they appear, make a habit of asking first-time visitors: "How did you happen to hear about us?" The answers form patterns very quickly.

Make the question casual: "Did you see our ad in the *Cricket* yesterday? We thought people would like to know about our early raspberries."

Keep track of the yeses and noes, because you should be ready to try another method if you are getting poor results. But if you've done it right, from choosing the medium to writing the copy, the responses may be unexpectedly pleasing.

What to expect. Sometimes you can go for weeks with nary a sign of results from advertising, but it is silly to get disturbed if you don't get a big response. In mail advertising, if you get a 6 percent return (the people you mail something to, mail something back), you're doing very well. Other methods can bring smaller results—though every bit helps. I guess that's why advertising costs so much. You can put your market's name before 5,000 people, but if 300 say they saw it in the paper, then you invested supremely well.

What to say. However your ad is to get to the public, build it on a clear idea. You might list the advantages of carefully grown fresh foods, or no harmful chemicals on your fruits (if that is true), or suggest your market for a country jaunt. And never close any ad without clear directions for reaching your market. Never close a spoken ad without a thank you.

Ads and commercials (and your thoughtfully planned displays) can bring many sales when you build them around appealing ideas. Go to your extension agent for more ideas to build a campaign around. Also see the promotional ideas in Chapter 9.

SHOTS IN THE DARK: RADIO ADS

Radio advertising, too, can get news of the market to the buying public, though some may think the cost is a little hard to justify when you're just getting into the business. Spot commercials 30 or 60 seconds long can get a good-sized message over. The cost may keep you from advertising more than a few times during the growing season, yet those few could be enough. Try an opening-date announcement, then advertise again when you'll be harvesting your biggest crops. For a third try you might decide to prime the profit pump with news of a special sale.

Radio is a direct way of getting at potential customers' ears, though for every hundred people who hear your ad, you might be lucky to get one to come into the market. That's why you should find out how many ears the broadcast will reach. Fall back on your special appeal by injecting a quiet, modestly worded spot among the shrieking commercials and howling rock music.

How to say it. Read your local paper closely and listen to the local radio to see the timing, style, and content of other people's produce ads. How do your ads compare? Yours probably will be all the better for not sounding slick and professional. Let other people copy the supermarket advertising. It really isn't suitable for the roadside audience for the most part. Leave the huckstering to the people who need it because they haven't your advantages. And for

---

SAMPLE RADIO SCRIPT

WHP-HARRISBURG, PA.

5000 ON 580

ASHCOMBE VEGETABLE FARM

(30 SEC) WED., OCT. 2

YOUR FAVORITE FALL EATING APPLES ARE
ONLY $1.50 PER HALF BUSHEL AT ASHCOMBE
VEGETABLE FARM . . . . CHOOSE FROM
"JONATHAN," "GRIMES," "GOLDEN
DELICIOUS," AND "RED DELICIOUS."
ASHCOMBE'S HAVE APPLE CIDER, BY THE
GALLON . . . . WINTER SQUASH AT $1 PER HALF
BUSHEL . . . PIE AND JACK O'LANTERN
PUMPKINS, TOO. THAT'S AT ASHCOMBE
VEGETABLE FARM, A SHORT FIFTEEN-MINUTE
RIDE FROM HARRISBURG ON THE GRANTHAM
ROAD AT WILLIAMS GROVE. OPEN WEEKDAYS
TIL NINE. CLOSED SUNDAYS.

---

heaven's sake—*no* singing commercials. The best reason for
not making that mistake is that everyone else is doing it.

Cost. The spot you buy can be inexpensive if you stay off
the high-pressure parts of the dial. Highlight the fruits and
vegetables now in season with a simple, direct message
describing them, telling the market's name and special
character, and spelling out directions on how to reach you.
(See the sample script above.) Mention extra services that
you offer. Watch out for talk of prices, though, because there
you call down on yourself comparison with discounters'
offerings. Normally, prices won't be one of your strongly
competitive points, but bargain prices are another story.

Time your ads and play up the country image. Set up radio or newspaper ads for your peak selling days, which will almost always be on weekends when more people are on the roads, with their car radios tuned for helpful news of where to shop. Plan your advertising mostly for those weekend shoppers, easing them away from competitors. Then try a switch by offering special attractions to the people who'd rather drive on less crowded weekday roads, and you may manage to spread your sales over the week *and* increase them.

You can pull people to your market with quiet but magnetic advertising. And always remember the advantages you offer—freshness, ripeness, naturalness, friendly service, and a country setting. Offer all this in a low-key, informal style, not the hammer-and-tongs commercialism that big marketers seem convinced is the winner-take-all way.

SELLING THROUGH THE TUBE

Another good puller is television. You may find a station close enough and inexpensive enough to get your message around. It seems worth trying once, perhaps for your opening announcement. But you'll probably have to go through an advertising agency. It isn't easy to dream up, write, illustrate and produce a videotape script for a really small business, even for a 30-second spot. But then, hang the cost—why leave all the selling time to those big moneymakers?

DIRECT MAIL

For direct mail advertising, another way to attract customers, you might use the commercial trick of buying a list of names at so much a head, as the big advertisers do. But you should not need anything like this. If you're simply mailing an announcement that the market is opening, or that first corn will be ready June 30th, all you need are the names and addresses of regular customers, friends and local businessmen.

A reliable way of getting your own mailing list is to have a *guest register* near the front of the market where people are asked to fill in their names and addresses—so you can let them know when you're harvesting something they're interested in, or are having a sale, or a pick-your-own special.

A book sitting there and simply called "guest register" isn't enough. You've got to offer something to get people to hand out their names and addresses. Many will want to sign up if they know the reason for it, though, and everyone working in the market should be reminded to ask their customers to sign the register to receive announcements.

Use a postcard. It's most economical to keep your mailed messages to a simple postcard. And a card can be striking in its own way with a little drawing to go with the message. Keep the wording short.

Writing or typing the message, preparing a stencil and running off copies, addressing and stamping the cards all takes time. Think about investing in a copying machine—later, perhaps—and maybe a postage meter. But you can start simply with a batch of postcards and a typewriter—or a willing helper with a clear hand.

Direct mailings are another duty that can be assigned to a family member as a regular way of helping out. An ingenious helper will find ways to make interesting mailings, appealing enough at first glance so they won't be discarded unread. Make them simple, personal, tasteful and informal.

Apples
Less then 3 lbs 29¢ a lb
Unit Price
29 a lb
3 lbs - 79c
26 1/3
4 lbs - $1.00
25 a lb
Special
1/2 bushel - $2.95
15 1/2 ¢
1 bushel - $4.95
macon
$1.00

Chapter 8

Advertising on the Spot

The customer is in your hands with the produce before him. What else can you do to improve the chances of getting his money into your register?

It comes down to the displays you've prepared—if they're a little better than simple stacks with the price on top. True, the food cries out its own advantages. But you can equip the market itself to help in the final selling push. Home-made display signs don't have to be much different from those you'd see in any other roadside market—hand-painted pictures of the fruit or vegetable explaining which price and quantity goes with which item, cards identifying varieties of items and their relationships with other varieties; recipes, posted nearby on clearly typed and duplicated sheets suggesting multiple and unusual ways of serving old familiars; illustrated signs showing off the beauty in freshly grown foods and flowers; color photographs blown up to large sizes showing parts of the farm and your equipment in operation and the crops at different stages ("from bare ground to green glory in so many weeks").

Alice keeps the scales near to hand for customers' convenience.

SALESMAN WITHOUT WORDS

Display advertising or point-of-purchase selling—it doesn't matter which you call it—is the silent salesman on which a lot depends. It means showing off your produce as flatteringly as you can manage, and getting it to show up brightly.

It's impractical to drag every customer by the hand to each of your products. Instead, you design your displays so that they will do all that without human help. Once the people walk into the market, they are, after all, a captive audience. While you've got them, use every second to lead them to the point of it all—exchanging money for produce. You got their attention long enough to draw them in; now help your salespeople by setting up displays that will touch up the whole effort. Dress up each display, whether table top, bin, dump table, wall shelves, refrigerated cabinets, or skids of picking-display trays. Each well-planned display will have a chance to stop the customer for a moment and stimulate him to buy. Now you and your produce join with that other salesman, impulse, to make your work pay off.

You'll need a three-step program to get all pulling toward the sale. These ideas were touched upon also in my section on planning the market in Chapter 3.

First, put everything together for *eye appeal.* Is every fruit and vegetable clean, unblemished, polished if necessary to look sparkling fresh and at its ripened peak? Is all your equipment, from counter tops to floor, neatly painted and spotless? Is the packaging adequate and does it complement, not hide, what's inside? Do you have an interesting *variety* of foods to offer? Are all displays orderly and placed with contrasting colors next to each other, showing no holes where customers have cleaned you out? Is the food's beauty enhanced by lighting and shade, graduated in size, grouped by uses, and safe from the sun's overheating? Now that you're facing customers who may formerly have known you only by your advertising, everything has to be in its place, watched constantly for excellent appearance.

Second, have you designed the market with plenty of space around everything that people want to be near, so that customers don't have to squint at you across a broad expanse of counter or wander among haphazard displays, spending time on the less profitable merchandise and passing up the things that can bring your best income? Are small items carefully packaged for easy picking up, undamaged, and ready for instant sale?

Third, is it easy to see, get near, even touch everything you have for sale? Are all products (especially the less familiar ones) clearly identified and marked with price and quantity? Are your specials in the most obvious places where they'll appeal immediately to people walking through, but shrewdly spread so that they won't be the only things visible? Have you planned how everything will be rotated as you refill each display, removing things gone by their prime and bringing the aging things to the center of each display and the new stuff farthest from reach?

Is everything that is meant to move in working order and everything that sits, solid and unbroken—racks, shelves, bins, tables, counters, refrigerated cabinets? All this equipment is just as important as production machinery. (Re-read the maintenance tips in Chapter 4.) It must be easy to load up with produce, to move to where you want it to be, to change and rotate displayed produce on, to sell and buy and bag from, and to clean up between fillings. All the display fixtures ought to be adaptable to displaying more than one kind of produce in more than one way. We went over fixtures in the section on equipping the market in the first place; now that the market's in action you can re-evaluate them.

Adaptability is vital in a small market or a big one. Labor-saving is next in value. You'll want to be able to set up and knock down displays fast and without trouble—to change them during the selling day, and get them ready to go in the morning, as well as put away at night. With room for plenty of displays and a loading and preparing area out of the public's way, plus equipment on wheels for getting to and from the back room, you can keep things moving as fast as crops come in and are emptied from the displays by customers. If the sun gets in, you can move the most sensitive items out of its heat. Of course, that means the floor has to be smooth enough to roll things around on, and walls and doors are placed to make moving the displays easy and safe.

The displays should be roomy enough to hold anything from the smallest fruits and berries to the biggest squashes, plus bags or boxes full of produce. Every part has to be sturdy to stand lots of heavy loads and much banging around, but short enough to keep everything within easy reach of customers and helpers.

With deliberate choosing, all equipment will be close to maintenance-free, having a durable, easy-to-clean finish all around. Whether you build the equipment yourself or buy it used out of supermarkets closing down, make sure you check it daily or weekly for breakdowns, then add a fresh coat of paint twice a season or so.

A market that has exceptionally quick turnover only at the season's peak may need refrigerated displays, with ice or other cooling equipment. Besides the high cost, gas or electrical cooling makes you sacrifice some of your uncommercial atmosphere. Still, holding fresh quality and cutting spoilage can mean a lot to you in profits.

Flow charts. When your business grows big enough that you feel a little helpless about ways of being more efficient, and you need help planning your displays, consider the flow charts prepared by Ransom A. Blakeley that we have included in Chapter 3. Experience told him that customer and helper traffic in any market big enough to walk around in can be a problem but also a tool for the marketer. He sat down and plotted customers' comings and goings, and he suggests that you do the same. Spend a little time in the market simply tracing people's moves from outside, to displays, to cash register, and out again. Record each customer's path (for perhaps a dozen of them), and then combine all the paths on a sheet of tracing paper, showing every piece of equipment at its present position. This simple trick can tell a lot about your physical layout. It helps answer the question *Where should I put everything?* Doing that correctly can make a big difference.

Any marketer who carries more than one kind of produce and has several displays will find people steering directly for the item that's most popular most of the time. That might be corn. Leave it up to the people and they may not go near other vegetables, particularly the less glamorous beets or potatoes. Many customers do come in for just one item. They might take an extra step for a free cold or hot drink, but unless they are regulars who care about freshness in all the things they eat, other items may be ignored. A flow chart will almost surely show ways of placing things to get people to notice everything in the market. You can also make your helpers' movements more efficient, which means customers will get better service, and everyone will be less tired from unplanned movements.

Can you tell just how effectively you've laid out the market before you have any customers? I doubt it. The real test will be watching carefully on one of your busiest days. Then flow charts are a useful, mechanical way of judging if you could do better. The important questions for a market-to-be are: Which place is best for each item you sell? For the display unit it will sit on? And above all, Where will the best-selling items go?

The last is easiest to figure out—spread the crowd-pleasers around, not symmetrically in the four corners but sprinkled among all the items; not up front where people can buy one thing and get on their way, but back among the things less in demand, such as the staples. Grouped varieties can be off on their own, for their own special appeal, but intersperse big sellers with steady ones, to gently move the people around to foods they need but can find nearly as fresh and maybe cheaper at the supermarket. Everything has to be given maximum exposure, which is what lies behind the appealing look in successful markets. Give every product its best showing, assuming you're eager for a balanced income with all you grow or sell.

Everything Counts

Just as you have to be constantly aware to keep unit costs down on every kind of produce, so each item ought to pull its own weight in your sales picture. Remember that your fixed costs don't change, whether a customer buys one item or six at your market. The more you can convince him to buy, the lower your cost per unit sold will go.

Make a layout. A *preliminary* guesswork flow chart which you may have prepared earlier by watching people in someone else's market (see Chapter 3), can be made into a plan for apportioning the market into (1) selling space and (2) functional space. These break down into displays, aisles, checkout, unrefrigerated and cold storage, special promotional displays, and preparation area. Most important are the selling and display sections. Much of your space should be set aside for that. Try to plot alternative traffic plans.

Here's one fanciful possibility: People come in close to an attractive floral display next to a table piled high with fruits, some of them bagged and ready to be carried to the checkout. On they go to cooler bins of corn in bags also ready to be sold. Past there is the salad display, with several kinds of greens, cherry tomatoes and beefsteaks, Bermuda onions and scallions, celery, watercress, and perhaps home-made salad dressing or the makings for it (oils, vinegars, spices). Then comes a mixed vegetable counter with root vegetables—beets, carrots, beet greens, turnips; then bins or tables with potatoes, squashes (of as many varieties as you can grow), cooking onions, snap beans, mushrooms, and so on through your catalog of good things to eat. The order doesn't matter so much as breaking the produce up a lot. Intermingle lower-priced, less glamorous vegetables and flowers in varying sizes and types of containers.

⋅ Next can be tables with items marked to be sold in larger quantities for freezing or canning—fruits or vegetables. A side collection of materials to be used for freezing or canning is a convenience and a profit-maker if you can buy the equipment at a reasonable discount: jars, lids, cookers, tongs, strainers, freezer containers and plastic wrap, and a box of free recipes and instructions for all kinds of preserving. Finally, the checkout.

Planning carefully, you can pick an arrangement that will run customers through in more or less the sequence you prefer, with signs to help guide them. No, they won't care to be run 'round the path more than once, except by choice.

Displays look most enticing fully stocked, even in the early morning when crack-of-dawn shoppers stop in on the way to work or to take kids to school, or the late birds on the way home in the evening. Roger Ginder mentions that some will try to come early to get first choice of everything before the foot-draggers pick it all over. Later, with experience in shopping at your market, they will know that things are freshly replenished all day long. For a few minutes' wait, regular visitors can be told the next batch is due in about now, if some of their choices happen not to have been restocked. Little attentions like that will bring them back more often.

Once you have an arrangement that works, try to keep it that way all season, a convenience that regular customers will appreciate because they can get in and out faster even if the market is crowded. Break up all the displays by colors, sizes, and textures, in bulk and bags and baskets. The baskets give a fancy touch and help fill the displays. In them you can most effectively show tomatoes, apples, peaches, pears, onions, potatoes, and peas. Keeping things varied like this is proof that you have a lot of variety and a well-stocked market; that you have almost everything fresh that they need in one shopping place, and above all that there is good turnover.

The Package Is a Salesman, Too

Important to consider as you're planning displays is the kind of packaging (if any) that's right for each kind of produce and every kind of display—like the touch that baskets can give. All this takes time, though you can save some (and money, too) by getting all packaging materials from one supplier.

Price is your biggest worry in packaging. Self-service containers cost a lot less than reusable types, even less than transferring merchandise from the lasting containers into paper bags or cartons when the customer is ready to buy.

Food that's already in a carry-home package helps push that impulse sale over the edge and moves the selling faster, and labor costs go down as speed goes up. Physical damage is cut down by prebagging too, because last-minute handling at the hurried checkout is omitted.

Using the one-way containers like miniature shopping bags in several sizes (and made of sturdy kraft paper with a trustable handle) gives you a place also to stamp or print a bit of advertising on the side, an inexpensive, convincing commercial.

The market's name and your logotype is enough to have

printed if you don't want to bother with the selling message. To cut out the expense of printing, you can have a rubber stamp made and ask a family member to stamp up the containers.

Sell colors. It may sound far-fetched, but choosing colors for your packages can enhance the natural beauty in your produce. The colors should *complement* those of the fruits and vegetables, not match them. Pick pastel shades, not bright colors. The food's colors, spread in a swath on tables at the market's front, make a display in themselves, perhaps visible from the road. Plastic mesh baskets help display small fruits and berries. You can see through them but they still are protected against handling. These plastics aren't perfect because they cost more than paper or pasteboard and aren't yet biodegradable.

Packages come in endless varieties of shape and color. Two sizes are good for a start for the fruits—one for eating-sized quantities and a bigger one for preserving. One or two-quart boxes and baskets are good for traveling. Four-quart, eight-quart, and 16-quart sizes are most popular for larger fruits and vegetables. But be sure all the sizes are standard, easy to know by sight to avoid costly confusions on busy days. Keep all packages in each display the same size. It looks better and makes it easier for customers to tell just how much they want. Careful packaging keeps order in the market, cuts handling, makes produce look beautiful with no misrepresenting, can be prepared in advance, helps keep food fresh, and, after you're done with the sale, makes easy, protective carrying for the customer. Chosen with sense, packages cut handling cost, and this keeps prices down and sale quantities up.

Self-baggers. The packages you pack fruit in may be as simple as small white bags for a pound or two or several bunches of grapes, or the big kraft bags for half-bushels of potatoes or apples. Kraft comes in all sizes and colors and several weights. If you don't ready-bag the produce, keep piles of bags handy as part of each display. One efficient marketer I know hangs rolls of tear-off plastic bags over his shelves and bins next to the customer scales.

Other self-service containers are the familiar but expensive wooden veneer baskets and the corrugated cardboard boxes with handles, which cost less and are just as rugged. But then, if you're small enough not to worry about niceties like packaging, the bulk display and merchandise packed in a plain brown bag (by customer or you) may be best. It is simpler, more countrylike, and needs less of an investment. It's only when growth makes you move produce faster that you may have to spend more to earn more.

If your market is between smallest and medium size, try both ways and wait for experience to tell which way you should go. Unless you have a gigantic bug problem, keep covers off any and all containers. Plastic sheet does protect against insects and dust, but it also makes things age faster (unless they're in refrigerated displays). It also gives a mass-produced look. The only time to cover everything up is if, after closing or before opening, you spray the whole market to keep the wildlife down.

You also can box or basket the produce for a more fetching look, but if it's feasible put the produce in a bag inside the other container so that you can simply lift it out when the customer brings the whole thing to you at purchase time. Transferring food from the attractive basket into an old bag may bring an "Aw, I thought the basket went with the fruit." Then you simply mention the retail price the empty basket sells for. That may change the "aw" to an "ow." But it might also bring in a little extra profit if you've done your buying carefully. Baskets and attractive boxes are necessary for fruit gift packs, as house gifts, and for many other times that call for a real present (See Chapter 9).

What else can a package do? Packaging, if you do any, is such an important part of the growing business that the review put together by Ransom Blakeley is sure to be handy. He suggests that for anything you sell by volume instead of weight, the self-measuring package does that job and others too. It protects produce against physical damage—bumping, squashing, and squeezing, as well as the heat built up by direct sunlight. It keeps out contaminants, too, such as rain, dust, dirt, and bugs. And, if it's chemically treated, it can preserve produce from mildew. The package also does the customer some favors: It lets him see the produce right through it, displaying the full beauty of your crops. It protects easily damaged food all the way home, where it is handy for storage and even for serving. It reminds him where the product was bought and for how much (when you mark the price right on the package). It may even tell how to use the contents if instructions are applied. Some containers can be recycled, too—used over and over in the home.

Other types of packages are useful to know about. When you sell cider, you can use paper cartons, which take up little space, or squared plastic jugs that fit on the refrigerator shelf, though neither shows the cider in its true color. The *pallet box* is good for bulk displays. You pick right into it and then move it with a fork lift (attached to a tractor, if you don't have a separate one) from the field to the market, where it acts as a bulk display case. A *tote tray* works in the same way with quart boxes packed in it. Wooden trays hold dry produce; plastic or plastic-lined trays handle the wet stuff. In

this way you harvest, transport, store, restock, all with the same trays, also saving the produce from extra handling.

Mr. Blakeley warns not to pile displays so high that they obscure other displays. But enough height also is important, so that people don't have to stoop to see the merchandise. Try to get everything between eye and knee height. Make things easy to reach by avoiding step displays. A display table should be shallow enough so that people won't have to reach more than two feet to get anything on it.

Chapter 9

Add to Your Market—and Prosper

TRY SOMETHING NEW

What about other ways of adding volume? The methods we've looked at for selling more produce and making higher profits are a beginning, but others have been tried with some success. We'll look at those next, but not before considering a criticism R. Alden Miller passes on. Many marketers have a way of leaning *too* heavily on the high quality they grow into the things they sell, and on the excellent service they give all customers. They neglect one vital habit successful retailers build for themselves—using canny promoting to convince present and future customers that they need more of what you sell than they thought they did.

Then why not try new lines of produce that you may have neglected for one reason or another? "Nobody ever asks for it around here," (it may be that no one told them there was such a thing); "It's too hard to grow without such and such" (all the more reason for growing and selling something exclusive, for which you can charge uncompetitive prices).

First, try new ways of selling merchandise you already carry, promoting it to bigger profits, of course. It may seem like a lot of bother. You say your imagination isn't good enough? Then take what you find here if it fits. We publish these suggestions just to get you thinking up newer and better ones.

161

Remember this from Siles B. Weeks: Your costs for location, building, and labor—your overhead—mostly are fixed. By being more efficient you might shave them a little, but they're still there. Any sales that you can add to the ones you're chalking up already will go directly into building your net income. And promotion of one sort or another is a way to make that extra sale.

Also remember that Roger Ginder said the more people you bring in, the lower your cost for each of them, if they buy something.

Sell More Corn

A good place to begin promoting your way to better profits is right in the corn patch. (Please look back at the data on handling and storing corn in Chapter 4.) Corn is the biggest seller for many markets, (see Chapter 3), and generally it doesn't need much extra salesmanship to move it out of the market and into the customers' pots. But what about midway through the season, when corn two or three times a week has gotten a little tiresome? That's the time to give it the extra push that will sell even more and keep it from piling up in displays and storage places. It's also your job now to keep the price high enough to add profits instead of cutting them to where you'd rather give the stuff away. Try selling corn two dozen for the price of one, once a week, as a kind of loss leader that really won't lose you anything, because it may bring more people to buy. That's one way of getting an overwhelming surplus crop moving. Change the day you offer this bargain every week, so that it won't get to be too much of a good thing.

How many ways is corn good? R. Alden Miller says that about half the vegetable acreage in his part of New England is in sweet corn, and when the hot weather comes, bunched plantings let it loose on the market all in a heap at harvest time. This is a good reason, then, to tell everybody all about corn and the many ways to use it. Since Pilgrim times, after the Indians taught the immigrants how to grow corn, it has

The corn isn't all up front, so that people will step inside for other purchases, let's hope.

been a healthful, delicious, proteinful favorite, eaten (for all we know) raw, fresh and juicy right off the stalk, boiled on the cob or sliced off it, steamed or roasted in the husk, mixed with anything else the cook pleased in kernel form, and best with pure butter, some salt, and a smell of pepper. When you cut it off the cob, or scrape it to get every bit, corn can go into scalloped, succotashed, custarded, or puddinged dishes; put it in souffles, fritters with maple syrup on top, or stuff it into peppers, or build it into soups or chowders. It can go into relishes too, and, as immature kernels, into pickle mixes.

The New England Regional Extension Service can send you *Cooks in the Cornpatch,* a booklet with recipes that will make even *your* corn-sated glands salivate, and will help you sell more of this food that has nourished people since before we discovered the Old World. Miller talks of giving corn roasts late in the season, and how many people are delighted to find that fresh corn can be had after most growers give up on it for the season. Like early corn, after the long winter, late corn can earn a name for itself. You can help revive people's taste for fresh corn by growing and advertising late-season harvests, so that people can eat it or preserve it for the oncoming winter and not have to resort to supermarkets' antique varieties. Having some ears cooked, ready to eat, and *free* is a powerful way of promoting corn for some extra profits.

Because corn is popular with everyone, you can stock gimmicks that people like to buy inexpensively from you (instead of expensively in gift shops). Cornholders and cornpicks make it easy to eat, tongs save tender fingers from quick-boiled ears, and a special plunger can get the butter on the right place without sullying fastidious fingers. You could even stock special corn knives and cornbowls for corn the way I remember my grandparents had to have it, sliced off the cobs and floating in butter, the right way for people running low on original teeth.

ADD SPECIALTIES

Blueberries. Promotion doesn't have to be limited to the golden vegetable. Other crops deserve playing up too, like the *wild blueberry.* Homer B. Metzger and A. A. Ismail of the University of Maine Agriculture Experiment Station tested how fresh blueberries could be made into a locally grown and sold specialty. With a hardly noticeable promotional campaign they set up an experimental business marketing the fresh, wild berries at local roadside markets. They figured that (1) Maine ships in almost all its berries for local sale; (2) blueberries are a natural crop for the topography, more practical than most other fruits and berries; (3) picking and selling wild berries would help with jobs for pickers and profits for roadside marketers; (4) direct marketing would keep money in the state that usually was spent on imports mostly from New Jersey, North Carolina, and Michigan.

Most marketers welcomed the chance to sell fresh local berries. The only advertising they did was point-of-purchase signs and give-away recipes. The experiment was not a commercial success—it didn't make a profit. But it did prove the market is there, waiting for someone to go beyond the experiment with the efficiency that growers and roadside people certainly could supply. How about your area?

How about preserves? One product people expect to find at roadside markets fits right in with the home-grown, high-quality feeling—preserves of all kinds. Making some or all of them in your own home from cultivated fruits and vegetables or, better still, relatively cost-free wild berries, you can add a small but steady chunk to your income. Some people sell nothing *but* preserves at their markets. Gene Logsdon talks in *Farm Journal* (March, 1972) of two ladies who started a stand selling jams and jellies, offering specialties like gooseberry preserves, wineberry jam, currant jelly, wild raspberry preserves, elderberry jelly—in all 42 varieties of jams, jellies and relishes! They use wild berries when they can and have sold as many as 250 half-pint jars in a week.

Some people combine preserves with local honey, mixing the displays among vegetables and fruits. Backlight both jellies and honeys if you can, using their subtle colors to beautify the market and draw people to them. You will have to learn the laws on selling preserved food to the public

(check your state Department of Agriculture), and you'll want to find the best sources for materials, including containers. If you have to, supplement local berries and other fruits with shipped-in varieties.

Try to find container suppliers close by, preferably *not* big commercial manufacturers. If this project is too time-consuming, have a group of neighbors share the work and profits. You supply materials, they put in the time, and put their own names on the jars. "Especially Prepared for the Family Market by Neverfresh Products, Brooklyn, N.Y." may not bother passersby, but regular customers want something local, no matter how good the commercial kinds may be.

Greenhouse delicacies. Long-springed years too wet and cold for early crops are perfect for early greenhouse tomatoes, especially with the high yields you can get. Plastic greenhouses, not very expensive to set up and maintain, can give you a salable crop when tomatoes will sell best—in the early spring. Who wants to eat those hard, tasteless, greenpicked imitations masquerading as fresh, ripe, to-matoes in the supermarkets? They are poor competition for really fresh, vine-ripened fruit from your own greenhouse. Plastic greenhouses can allow a very early opening and late closing for your market, and win you profits from other roadside markets restricted to the regular growing season and from retailers who have nothing to sell but shipped-in produce. If your extension service doesn't have plans for greenhouse culture you can get bulletins on this subject from the USDA in Washington.

DECORATOR VEGETABLES

Robert Stevens has another idea that ought to spread in these grow-it-yourself times: Sell people vegetables that they can grow like flowers on patio, porch or windowbox. They'll have the fun of growing the plants, enjoy the decoration they give, love the ease with which they can be grown, and lap up the freshness that makes good eating. You can hand out written-up instructions with each sale, and probably you ought to sell the fixings needed to grow the plants.

That's easier, of course, if you already carry garden tools and supplies. Prices can be higher than if you were selling the plants in nursery quantities, but still low enough to be a real bargain and an attractive, productive bit of greenery for the house. This can be a hobby for city dwellers, too; even people who live in apartment houses have windows in which to place the plants or can grow them under lights.

Gardeners want to spend. For that matter, you really can't afford to miss the current gardening explosion. Sell flats of seedling vegetables for an easy start in the back-yard garden. Keep seeds on hand, too, for the more enterprising gardeners. Carry plenty of equipment, including fertilizers, mulches, safe pesticides, tools (perhaps including spreaders and tillers for rent) and gardening books. You'll worry much less about garden enthusiasm cutting into your sales. The educational television series that help inexperienced gardeners also tell about all the equipment and materials they will have to lay out money for, which is where you can come in. Many people going in for home gardening learn to like fresh vegetables, too, which may eventually get them to your door. After all, they can't grow everything themselves, most of them anyway.

THINK ORGANIC:
SELL A PHILOSOPHY

Don't forget the organic side of the gardening movement. Be prepared and stocked with natural fertilizers that will be demanded by people who have acquired the taste for "naturally" grown foods. Robert Stevens suggests limestone, cottonseed meal, and bone meal, with, of course, plenty of dried manures. These items take up space but they please the truly interested organic gardeners who need them to supplement their compost.

The non-chemical fertilized and non-toxic and non-residual pesticided fruits and vegetables are the most important facts about organic growing. You may not be converted exclusively to the organic method yourself, but you'll get endless questions about it, especially if you (wisely) carry goods, foods, and information that these serious people want. If you *do* follow the organic precepts in your growing, you'll find many more people eager to buy your produce, even though they may know little about the method itself. The organic idea ties in beautifully with the natural, country appeal a true farm market must have, and it gives you another leg on the commercial marketers.

Fruits and vegetables that *can* be advertised as "organically grown" (by you or a special supplier) will bring premium prices. It is unlikely, however, that the full range of produce your market stocks could be "organic," and for that reason be careful in your advertising.

I won't try here to go into the techniques and economics of organic gardening, which is a big subject in itself, especially when applied to a market-garden-sized operation. Probably the best source of information in this field is Rodale Books, Inc., Emmaus, Pennsylvania.

FRUIT GIFTS

This is a side business for fruit-growers, or anyone in marketing who would like to try a richly profitable new line. It is not the easiest way to make the market grow, for it takes care and management and time.

We can learn a great deal about it from a talk that Erskine Zurbrugg called "My Experience with Gift Baskets" at the Farm Market Conference at Egremont, Massachusetts in 1974. I've summarized his helpful remarks as recorded by Ransom Blakeley, but you can get a copy of the whole thing from Purdue University.

In 15 years Mr. Zurbrugg built a fruit basket business that is selling in a 50 mile radius from a small town not far from Cleveland, Ohio. It is up to 12,000 baskets a year, without mail-order sales. He developed it from nothing, getting the idea from a basket he assembled and gave in gratitude for help after he had an accident.

He made up his mind from the start to use nothing but fruits of the highest possible quality—extra fancy and nothing less. Forget you have competitors, he says. Don't try to see how cheaply you can make the gift basket, but how much you can put in it. Think of the baskets as *gifts*. They are fairly expensive gifts, but people don't order them often, and many can well afford the price.

Mr. Zurbrugg calls his the *prestige baskets*. His reason for emphasizing their extra-specialness is that many people associate *fruit baskets* with donations to the poor, and that is the image he has to change. He does it by seeing that people are proud of the gift basket he prepares.

The baskets are made on order only, sold from samples in the showroom, and they require 24 hours' notice. Labels tell everything that's in the basket and the overall price. All the baskets up to $15 are all fruit; above that they start adding special jellies, cheeses, and other delicacies. They even have a $200 basket, complete with champagne, caviar and an electric fondue cooking set. Few of those get sold but they're good to have around in sample form just to make the $50 baskets look inexpensive.

The most popular basket sells for $15. Construction firm owners and other small businessmen are among the best customers. They like to give fruit baskets to other businessmen and to the suppliers and brokers they deal with.

Doctors who don't charge other doctors for services rendered to their families like receiving fruit baskets in return. What, after all, do you give someone who takes in $50,000 to $100,000 a year? Baskets worth $50 and up are their favorites.

Use the biggest apples you can find, Mr. Zurbrugg advises. Washington State is his choice. They are wastefully large and the flavor may be nowhere as good as that of his local Ohio apples. But they are impressively big and beautiful.

Mr. Zurbrugg uses Florida navel oranges, so big they look

like grapefruit. They're wasteful too, but he's not trying to take care of a family's food budget at Christmas. The idea is that the gift is going to make people happy. They'll get something they wouldn't at any other time of year, something they decidedly can't buy in any supermarket. He also puts in tangerines, tangelos, red and yellow Delicious apples, cheeses from Holland, chocolate from Switzerland, and jellies from Israel. The last three could be bought for less in American brands, and would be as good, but the foreign labels add something extra.

What's in it? Into each basket go seven varieties of fruit. They don't include pears or bananas except in hospital baskets, because left to sit several days, these will get over-ripe and people will feel the whole basket is spoiled—a lot of money wasted.

People are sending fruit baskets instead of flowers to hospital patients, at $7.50 to $10 a basket. For the patient whose diet forbids everything in the basket, it's still handy to have, because the fruits are fine gestures of friendship to pretty nurses, handsome doctors, and fellow patients. Grapes go into separate baskets with handles that will protect them; the grapes go on top.

The fruits are stacked with grapefruit at the bottom, for the stability of their extra weight. Other fruits are packed with colors alternating, held in place with transparent tape. In fact, it's almost impossible to build a fruit basket without tape. The pyramid would crumble at a nudge, and the fruit would be bruised. With cellophane around the top of the basket, you can't see the tape that holds things together inside.

The baskets that have the most fruit showing sell best, and open baskets are winners. Hampers filled with fruit are a best buy, Mr. Zurbrugg feels, but most of the fruit they hold doesn't show, and people don't go for something that can't be seen. Shredded cellophane is used to fill the holes and brighten up the package. Small, ready-made bows are cheap and easy to get, but when the one who gets the gift looks at it, the whole package is the thing that counts. Spend extra for big bows.

Who made me? When you send out a gift basket, make sure the recipient knows where it came from so that all the thought and quality you've packed in won't go unappreciated. The card should tell how to take care of the perishable fruit, and that it has to be used soon for best eating.

Markup and inventory. The markup used is 50 percent on the smaller baskets and 100 percent on the bigger ones. They figure out their cost from the fruit and other items and then add the markup. Inventory control is vital, especially with the fancy non-fruit items, because no one wants to tie up a lot of money on overbought caviar that has to be held a whole year till the next major selling season. When ordering fruit and baskets, last year's business is used to gauge the needs.

Basket sources. The baskets are bought from an importer, ordered early because he has only two shiploads coming in a year. Mr. Zurbrugg gets his baskets from Yugoslavia—they are sturdy, and he finds Mexican baskets are too soft and don't hold up under the heavy fruit. He buys only baskets that will expose the fruit.

Delivery. Mr. Zurbrugg's company delivers gift baskets within a 15 mile radius, charging extra for the service. He has had poor luck with shipping or mailing baskets, except through United Parcel Service. Delivery services that charge a flat rate and will make repeat delivery tries are best, because often around Christmas people aren't home to get the packages, and the fruit can't sit around outside.

The cellophane used is 40 inches wide, even for the small baskets, and is wrapped from the bottom all the way around the top and back down. Tape, cellophane and other supplies have to be ordered three to four months in advance, because people just don't stock large quantities of them. Even though Mr. Zurbrugg sells most baskets in the three weeks around Christmas, he's in business all year and has to keep stocked up. He operates on cash only, except for the larger companies. Telephoned orders call for great caution, he warns, unless you know the purchaser.

Advertising is done mostly by word of mouth. The person who gets a gift himself is a potential giver for next year, and that simple fact has doubled and redoubled the business. Newspaper advertising hasn't worked because the purchaser has to see the package. The "poor basket" image still hangs on.

Showing his baskets at a local country club, for businessmen and their families, cost $1,500, but it brought in $10,000 worth of sales. The party was much more effective than any mass media advertising, Mr. Zurbrugg feels, because he was dealing with a select group of people.

The market. You have to be in a good marketing area to make this kind of business go. Roadside marketers will do little immediate business across the counter, but if friends learn what you have they'll spread the word. They find many occasions are right for giving fruit baskets—big occasions for business acquaintances, for bosses, employees, hospital patients, anniversaries for anyone, and a death in the family. The last two bring in most of the off-season business.

OPENING EARLY?
SELL PLANTS

You have to consider several things to get produce ready for sale much earlier than the other fellow can. The most successful markets specialize in having crops on sale before anyone else does, for which they get a premium price. If you get into this, of course you pay a price too, because you'll need a greenhouse or at least a combination of hotbeds and cold frames. And once you have those, why not go in for selling plants to brighten life for winterworn customers?

A word of caution about selling flowers and nursery stock comes from Robert Stevens. They are not easy to care for and will take a lot of time just when you're readying the market for opening day. And it's the same again at the end, when you may be eager to close up and get away. Right in the middle of your busiest (and maybe hottest) days, flowers and young plants will need still more care. Have you the time to keep them fresh-looking? How many varieties can you handle? Will you find enough demand, considering the competition you're bound to run into with big nurseries all around?

Getting started. It's best to start with a small stock for the first year, until you know how much you can profitably handle without upsetting the rest of your business. Mr. Stevens suggests ground-cover plants for easy maintenance, if you find any call for them. Myrtle, English ivy, pachysandra, and bugleweed are serviceable and salable possibilities, and evergreens and other trees, though they take more care, bring in good returns. You might keep only a small collection of bulbs because they are sold at a discount in many places. Chrysanthemums in pots sell well in the fall but need constant care to keep looking as they should. House plants are more delicate still.

Find a grower. If you don't want to or can't start bedding plants on your own (not having a greenhouse is a good reason), you should be able to find a grower who will supply you. Roger Ginder says you'll need an agreement with the grower on quantities, varieties, and dates of delivery before he begins to produce your order. If the plants are delivered early in the season (and they should be), you'll have to harden them off to condition them for the temperature they must live with at your market and in the customer's garden.
Here are some very good hints:

Supply yourself with growth regulator chemicals so that the plants will not grow too fast and tall. Along with the plants get printed labels with a picture of each plant as it will look in full bloom. These labels, more useful than a plastic chip with nothing but the flower's name on it, come from the seed companies and will even include the basic facts such as height when mature, spacing of rows, and when, where, and how to transplant.

Care. Protect the bedded plants from the wind, displaying them on sheltered tables, not on the ground or floor, to put them in better view. Cull sick or dying plants before they spoil your display. Be sure you know exactly what and when to feed the plants, what to give them if they look unhealthy, how to tend them when insects or diseases attack, and how much to water them. When you know all about them, you can also serve your customers better by instructing them on how to nurture these purchases. Building a reputation as a competent or even expert flower, tree, and bush grower can do nothing but good, even if you specialize mostly in selling edible, not decorative, plants.

Plantings around the market are the best way of displaying varieties that you sell. Some markets still sell flowers and display them most effectively inside, but leave the outside looking like a dump. Maybe a really efficient marketer hasn't time to worry about landscaping, but that's when the expert comes in handy. Invest in outside help if you can't do the planning or the work yourself. It may pick up business so much that you'll have more time or money to beautify your market.

Which varieties to sell? If you've done your homework before getting into bedding plants or nursery work, there won't be any doubt about which varieties look best, grow best, can be planted soonest and last longest, are easiest to tend, are biggest, smallest, prettiest, most adaptable, give best cover or most shade, are best for which kinds of soil, yield best fruit, are most attractive to birds and least appealing to pesky animals. You are expected to come up with a thousand facts, not as a seller of merchandise, but as an interested, experienced dealer. One simple but very important rule: Always put flowering varieties on display when they are blossoming. Doing all these things will keep your stock moving and leave you with few unsold plants at season's end.

It's possible, as more and more people seem to realize, to grow your bedding plants in artificial soil. In fact, it's easy to do and may be most convenient for some people. But Robert Stevens explains how much care it takes to grow flowers in this way, and how quickly they can lose their color, which is most of their appeal. The minimum to give these flowers isn't much to ask: (1) Give them a thorough daily watering. (2) If you hold any purchased plants more than a week, give them liquid food to make up for the natural nourishment they don't get in artificial soil. (3) Be sure you know just how much light each variety needs and place it to get no more or less. (4) Protect the plants against damaging heat, frost, sunlight, and wind. And sell them quickly.

Growing under lights. You may find the pleasure of growing plants under artificial lights will bring in extra income. It used to be a hobby mostly for wealthier people, but manufacturers have come up with small and portable units that will do the job in little space for small initial cost and not much extra on the electricity bill.

Read up on the subject of gardening under lights and set up a small demonstration corner. Stock a selection of the equipment—lighting fixtures and wood or metal display shelving, peat pots for starting seedlings, and books on the subject. Consider having kits on greenhouse units from window size or bulkhead (cellar door) types, to full-sized attached plastic and aluminum additions for a house or patio. These might not be high-volume sellers, but carry the new inexpensive types or even build-it-yourself plans to broaden the market's interest for many people. Year-round gardening isn't for everyone, but it's spreading, with an extra push from interest in vegetable gardening.

SELL A BUSH OR TREE

Be cautious about getting into the nursery business, selling bushes and trees as a sideline. The profits can be healthy, but you pay for them with lots of time, space, and work. Robert Stevens gives tips on handling these hardier (but still tricky) products: Evergreens (such as rhododendrons, junipers, yews, hemlocks and spruces) have to be canned or balled and burlapped while waiting for sale. They may need a special building or addition to the market to keep out drying and damaging wind, with a slatted roof to bring in lifegiving light. It's best to keep the stock in beds, surrounding them with peat moss or sawdust, watering the balls thoroughly. Be liberal with advice to customers, such as to plant the tree or bush with the top of the ball at ground level; mulching the plant to keep moisture in and weeds out; watering just once a week.

Carry the stock over. If you end your season with leftover nursery stock, Stevens adds, you'll have to mulch it, water it, feed and shade it, watching all the time for pests and pruning for health and beauty. This is where a lot of the extra care comes in, for nursery stock absorbs labor during the season and between seasons, not to mention caring for the plantings in your fields.

You must feed the plants regularly when you have them prepared for display (or two pounds of water-soluble fertilizer for 100 gallons of water every two weeks). When you're a couple of weeks away from the new selling season, Stevens says, feed them 3 or 4 pounds of "nugreen" in every 100 gallons of water to get the foliage to its best greenness. Watch regularly for pests like spider mites, aphids, or any of the countless bugs that eat plants and profits. Your county extension agent has help for you against these problems.

Branch out with seedlings. Seedling bushes and trees make another profitable sideline. Stevens says that unlike the big nursery businesses, you can sell them in small quantities to beautify smaller yards. Like their bigger relatives, they are not easy to store, but you can handle that by potting them in soil in small containers. The tiniest seedlings—no more than twigs—will bring a dollar or two each, and they're worth it. To get a good markup, though, you have to have them potted, which makes each sale quicker and easier than getting them out of the ground.

Stevens also stresses that it is a popular convenience for customers to stock mulches along with the trees, flowers, shrubs, or vegetable plants. All of them need good mulching. Mulches are not cheap, which means you'll have to shop. Most popular, according to where you live, are salt hay from the coastal marshes, tree bark, and peat moss. The biggest problems in carrying mulches are their price and bulkiness. Some of them come from far away and, being bulky, carry high freight rates. Others have to be reaped and packed like any other crop. Even those which are otherwise useless by-products cost more than many want to pay, yet all are so useful that they're worth the price to the serious gardener.

PROMOTE THE SEASON

Taking advantage of something as natural as the changing seasons is no more than you'd expect of a down-to-earth farm producer and market operator. After the big push in the spring and the busily producing summer, the much-publicized fall harvest season is the next big time for speeding up the promotion engine. While visitors mass the country highways pursuing the brightened landscape, you can draw in many of them as new customers by decking out the market with the traditional colors and objects of autumn.

Lou Albano encourages people to put the market in autumn dress, with pumpkin people built up from cornstalks and dressed like farmhands, flanked by shocks of corn and beckoning to all who pass on the road. He makes a cornucopia by tying husks to a hoop, tassel sides out, loading it as a "corn-of-plenty" with produce overflowing from its mouth. He dresses his own market with jugs of cider and suggests a cider barrel with spigots, advertising a free drink of cool cider for a hot fall drive (keep the cups small—you want to whet the taste, not quench the thirst). Once the people are enticed inside, please them with small but good free apples for the undersized shoppers—happy children make relaxed spenders of their parents. Start customers off with satisfying visits in the fall and good farm-produced food will keep them on the track next spring.

The pull of memories. A touch of nostalgia helps, too. Farm marketers are fortunate in their business because they can use the strong pull of memories. Displays can remind older folks of winter days in snug farm kitchens or an animal-warm barn, and snowy roads through winter fields and unspoiled woods. Convey these by pictures or relics displayed on the walls, reproductions of Currier and Ives prints, and add to them the cider-apple-pumpkin colors, plus dried flowers all around, free (also small) drinks of coffee from an ever-hot pot, and even profit-making home-fresh doughnuts, though it would be foolish to try to out-doughnut the chains. Doughnuts made in the farm kitchen, fresh every day, plus pure fresh cider can be a strong attraction in autumn. Back up the fresh doughnuts with a frozen supply; they come back from the icy state so well that it's hard to tell the difference unless you eat both at once.

As long as we're piling up the attractions, one that appeals especially, says Roger Ginder, is ear popcorn that people can shell for themselves and pop over a home-fire. And with a good source of firewood, you can bring in plentiful profits, selling wood in bundles of a half-dozen two-foot split logs—scraps that might bring two dollars or more in the city today.

Gourds for color. The old standby, gourds dried and perhaps shellacked, continue to please house-decorating

people. Add to them Indian corn, bittersweet with its bright reddish-orange berries, and Japanese lantern flowers for fall displays that will decorate the market and make extra income.

Consider Stevens's thoughts about another attractive product—the dried flowers that can be made into fine arrangements. People make a hobby (some even make money) working with these natural things, turning out artistically pleasing products. Raising dryable flowers from seed is easy and fast. Start in June and have mature flowers in ten to fifteen weeks. Among the popular varieties are statice and sea lavender. Others are sunrays (Acroclinium), love-in-a-mist, globe amaranth, strawflower, and plumed celosia. And still more varieties dry attractively, Stevens says, but they need special care.

You can use small grains, too. He suggests collecting these, and other plants good for dried arrangements, from neighboring farms if you don't grow them yourself—wheat, barley, rye, and oats have shapely heads of grain, yet not so heavy that when mature they will fall. If you have to buy these, do it early in the season while they are still plants, not decorative merchandise. Of course you can expand your stock greatly by looking around your fields for wild ones. You might, if you haven't the time to do that, encourage customers to do it, charging a dollar an armload, perhaps. The beauty of weeds is that they don't have to be dried chemically; they do it themselves. But carry the materials that people need for drying showy flowers—silica gel, glycerin, and borax—and have books that tell how to do it.

Terrariums, too. One more flowery way of supplementing your market income is selling *terrariums,* which seem to hold their popularity. Customers find these beautiful miniature woodlands worth paying for, either ready-made or piece by piece. They like the small amount of care terrariums take. All you need is a small plant or several of them in a reusable glass container, like wide-mouth bottles, brandy snifters, aquariums, old-fashioned candy jars, goblets—anything to fit the little plants into along with the earth they grow in.

Other plants. Nurseries carry truly countless varieties of tropical and woodsy plants. A few more Robert Stevens mentions are small-lobed English ivy, fittonia, strawberry begonia, small ferns, and pepperonia. From the woods come partridge berries, mosses and lichens, violets, rattlesnake plantain, and pipsissewa. You might put together a few sample terrariums to show what a little ecosystem can look like. They'll be snapped up by adults and children, office-bound workers, invalids, old folks, apartment dwellers, and anyone else.

CHRISTMAS SELLING

By lengthening your season till Christmastime, you can stock another profitable line—Christmas trees and wreaths. Grow them to be sold as living trees, for people to plant outside after the holiday season. The high price you must charge for these trees keeps the market for them fairly small, but it can be steady, for killing a tree for the holidays doesn't strike everyone as the thing to do. People also realize they can have a grove before long by investing in a growing Christmas tree every year. Local growers charge about $15 for a table-high sized tree and $40 or so for a good-sized blue spruce that will (if the buyer is lucky and careful) hold up well under a full complement of ornaments, and then live in the yard when transplanted.

Cut-your-own trees. Some people grow Scotch pines and balsams for a cut-your-own Christmas tree trade. One enterprising and conservation-conscious farmer I know sells trees to families and throws in a seedling to replace the tree the family has cut (with guidance). The whole family gets in on the pleasure of tree picking and cutting, and they have the satisfaction of knowing their tree will be replaced.

Or you can ship Christmas trees in. Find out about sources from your extension agent. Pick one variety or carry some of each popular type—balsam and Scotch pine. Look into your source carefully so that you'll be sure to get enough trees of good quality, cut as close to Christmas as possible. Most of the trees sold in the East seem to come from far up in New

England and into Canada. All appear to be cut at about the same time—as early as September. That means they can't be fresh by Christmastime, no matter how cold it gets where they are cut. The National Christmas Tree Growers' Association (225 East Michigan Ave., Milwaukee, Wis. 53202) will send you a buyer's guide telling who distributes trees nearest you. The Association also supplies price tags with useful information printed on them, such as how to water the tree for safety and greenness. When you sell cut trees, explain to customers that even a cut-down tree makes more ecosense than plastic imitations.

Holly. Another holiday attraction you can sell is American, Chinese, and English holly plants, alive and plantable when the season is done. These sturdy, beautiful evergreens carry their own festoons of red berries and make fine plantings.

OTHER SEASONS, TOO

Rhododendrons, Stevens tells us, are a fine early season spring seller for Mother's Day. They are hardy evergreens and put on beautiful displays. *Azaleas,* too, are beautiful and popular, perfect for presentation at holidays or any special times. But the varieties have to be hardy enough for your climate.

Getting away from the holidays and back into midsummer, even the lowly earthworm can boost your profits a bit. If you're near good fishing streams, ponds, rivers, and lakes (and that covers most roadside markets) you'll find that putting up an unpretentious *"Live Bait"* sign among your others will draw extra customers. It wouldn't be wise to expect a large return from this sideline, but the beasts are easy to grow, especially if you can recruit neighborhood help to harvest nightcrawlers, hellgrammites, and minnows. The combination of bait and produce may seem weird, but Bill Osgood suggests this idea (along with many other possibilities) in his *How to Make a Living in the Country* (Garden Way Publishing).

SELL SERVICE TO PROMOTE
THE BUSINESS

Still on the subject of promoting as much business as you can, draw people's attention to the market and your produce by putting on special attractions, and by offering special services that will make the market known to lots of people. The more showy attractions will get attention, but the practical ones may bring sales.

Simple things like carrying the ladies' packages to the car without charge don't waste time—they win friends. If you can drop what you're doing to be helpful, and the helpers follow your example consistently, you're strengthening the market's image, and building a helpful reputation. Drinking water doesn't cost much, unless it cuts into profits you would make by selling cider or other fresh fruit drinks. Customer restrooms may be a nuisance but are also a great service. Or,

"Those are the best in the state," you can hear him say at Frank's Farmers' Market. A simple but appealing and well-visited open-air fruit and vegetable operation.

you might set aside a small area, partly in the sun and partly shaded, away from cars but visible from the market, where swings or playthings of wood, simple and safe, will keep children occupied for a few minutes. If your telephone is handy to the checkout, you might offer to take orders, to have them packed and ready for people to pick up. That and free local delivery for sizable orders could be strong points in your advertising.

Information. The *recipes* and helpful *how-to printed materials* that customers find appealing are easy to find and prepare. Put samples of these on a bulletin board, and keep copies within the customers' reach. Fill the selection out with cooking, canning, and freezing hints, all directly tied to the produce you carry. Much of that material can be gotten from your extension agent, free or at token cost. All you have to do is find a way of duplicating the material at low cost, and the agent may be able to help there too. The bulletin boards can be a useful service also for people who have something to sell or swap. Pick a time during your busy season and assign someone to set up a preparing and cooking demonstration to produce free samples. Consider also stocking good books for sale on these subjects.

Handing out recipes can be done effectively by tying them to separately displayed vegetables and fruits in large quantities, priced low. Put the recipes right in with the produce that's priced for stuffing the home freezer, and surround the displays with canning jars and lids. One thing you have to be careful of: if you gather recipes on your own instead of getting them from your extension service, be sure it's legal to distribute them to the public. You are making commercial use of them, which could be infringing on someone's copyright if they appeared in a published work. You can't simply go to the *Fanny Farmer Cookbook,* copy some recipes and hand them out, or you'll have the legal profession on your back.

PERIPHERAL PROFITS

People are earning a living running consignment shops full time, so that a self-running sale that takes little space and almost no selling time can do little harm. For running a "consignment corner" (displaying other people's keepables) you might keep 40 percent of the selling price, the owner of the goods getting the rest. Once the business is a little active, you may have to run a regular inventory, telling people to pick up things that haven't sold, sending out payment for things that did sell, and marking down others to speed their sale. This, too, can be an absorbing hobby, sometimes a moneymaker. At the least it is an extra bit of promotion. Having old things for sale, if the prices are fair and the items in good condition, can give the market atmosphere, too.

Animals. And speaking of atmosphere, you can make the market hard for children to resist by having a few animal pens. To be practical, they should be part of your working farm, though that may mean a little more smell than is good for the neat appearance you need (and flies, if you're not careful). Small pens, well tended and off a little way from the building, can give the kids who have never seen a farm in the flesh an interesting half hour—and get them to pull their parents out more often to do some buying along with the sightseeing.

Displays. Are you creative in setting up displays, and do you have extra space? R. Alden Miller suggests that you set up educational exhibits telling about the planning, work, and expense that go into growing produce. Include healthy specimens of what you grow, pictures of equipment that you buy or rent (plus price tags showing what they cost). Schedules for plowing, sowing, cultivating, and harvesting can be impressive. Show everything that you spend, with the cost per unit of a typical vegetable, covering chemicals (if any), fertilizers, farm and selling and preparation labor, containers and mortgage and taxes. Teach people that it's a business, not a gentleman farmer's hobby; that it takes a lot of work, financial investment, and care to make the earth give its bounty. Be sure you figure the costs on bulk quantities to avoid giving the wrong impression. Remember, most people never think beyond the supermarket counter about how their food gets made, except to complain about its cost, purity, or appearance.

Tourists. Vacationers and tourists can be a rich source of new customers for a market in or near a resort area, or a place with many second homes in which people spend time and money. Many of these are from the more affluent parts of the

186 Cash From Your Garden

population, and money you invest in appealing to them isn't likely to be wasted. Getting them to come is no easier, though, than reaching year-round residents. Welcome them back for the season with apt advertising and specially prepared sign language. They need fresh fruit and vegetables and also materials for landscaping, including flowers and other nursery products.

As M. E. Cravens says in *American Vegetable Grower* (June, 1973), it is often what you *give* and not what you sell that removes the limits to your volume and growth. The farmer's dozen, free slices of fruit for tasting, small but no-charge drinks, free parsley for dressing up the dinner plates—and all the other promotional ideas that you see in this book and in other people's markets are low-cost symbols of your generosity and eagerness to please. Offer a free pumpkin with a bushel of apples. Have an open-house day with free coffee, cider, and doughnuts, or run hayride tours of the farm for families by appointment or on selected dates at the season's height. Free pony rides or displays of farm animals, including baby animals that children can pet, are among hundreds of simple promotional ideas that will garner good will.

Food stamps. Are you near a city with low-income neighborhoods? You may want to be eligible to take food stamps for your produce. People getting this kind of assistance need fresh food as much as anyone else—perhaps more than most. You will have to file an application, then get your identification card and a kit explaining the food stamp program. Call your Department of Agriculture office.

PICK-IT-YOURSELF SALES

Maybe the most substantial way of adding appeal and profit to your market is starting a pick-your-own operation on sections of one or more appropriate and popular crops. Give your customers the choice—either buy it from the display or save cash and have healthful fun by doing the work

themselves. People who live in cities, including the children, are the most eager for a day out in the fields. They don't mind putting a little sweat and muscle work into a day's outing that might pay more in satisfaction than in savings.

How is it good for you? Public harvesting has clear advantages for you, too. Labor costs go down; you clean out surplus or leftover crops; and your grading, cleaning, sorting, packaging, storing costs—all your handling costs—drop away. It can bring in another kind of customer, too, the people who wouldn't ordinarily shop at farm markets for several reasons. Your regular prices, they may assume, are much higher. Then there's the trouble of getting to the market. They may even be unaware that the market is there.

"Pick-it-yourself" also cuts your spoilage, especially on tender crops, by reducing the handling they have to go through. Give the people a chance to do it themselves and they may engulf you in the rush, and then come back for more at the next harvest date. They'll pick produce that you might have a hard time selling, even over-ripe fruits you couldn't keep long enough to sell. They will pick unripe crops or fruit dropped on the ground. They'll strip your fields and trees bare, often buying more than they need. They'll stay all night if you let them, for harvesting has a fascination.

Ransom A. Blakeley and Morris S. Fabian, in *Pick-Your-Own Marketing: Selected Information and Bibliography* have much material on this type of selling, of which Extension Marketing, Rutgers University will send you copies. Many of the ideas you see here come from their suggestions.

Which crops? What should you grow especially for public picking? The inexperienced picker is best with the crops that mature all at once. Picking isn't easy work, so that the quicker the pickers' containers fill, the more it's worth to them, and the more you'll sell. Second, grow crops that are best when they ripen naturally in the field or orchard, not on the supermarket's shelves; or crops that don't ship easily because they are so tender, and just don't taste as good when they're picked green. People also like the crop that lets anyone know when it's ripe, usually by its size or color. Among the ones that farmers most often open up for pick-it-yourself are strawberries, raspberries, blueberries, cherries, peaches, apples, and pears. Plant the fattest, most luscious, quickest-ripening, most productive varieties. Some familiar pick-it-yourself vegetables are tomatoes, sweet corn, potatoes, peas, eggplant, lima beans, peppers, snap beans. Many others probably would go well with this kind of selling.

Waste no profits. One way of being sure that you're not losing the premium prices you could get by selling the crops only in your market is to pick the cream of the crop before opening the fields to the public. That makes sense, if only because many people expect lower prices on produce they pick themselves. Of course, leaving nothing but gleanings isn't going to attract many pickers, nor are they likely to come back again. The secret then seems to be offering quality just as good as you sell at the market, but keeping the pick-it-yourself and full-price areas completely separate. The steady pick-it-yourself customer is as important in this part of your business as the repeat customer is to your regular marketing business. Both deserve good value.

Disadvantages. Disadvantages in pick-it-yourself selling? Some there are, and the biggest is danger to the customer first and then to you. Let inexperienced people romp in fields and orchards, however big your troops of supervisors, and sooner or later you will find them doing horrendous harm to themselves, falling 15 feet from a tree and getting a (financially) large back injury. The hazards to their safety are not necessarily obvious. They hide in every crumbling furrow that can twist ankles.

One completely blameless accident that hits after years of perfect records can leave you more than saddened for the injury no one caused. It could wipe out your business unless you're covered by liability insurance. Do some consulting with the insurance agent long before you let people attack your fields and orchards. And be anything but skimpy about buying coverage.

Certainly you can take some precautions that will shrink the risks—of having accidents in the first place and of being ruined by them in the second. In fact, your insurance agent will insist that you do everything you can to cut the hazards, or else pay the price in premiums. Fabian and Blakeley mention a few ideas. First, get higher coverage than you think you'll ever need; it doesn't cost much more than the least you might get away with, but it might save your shirt and market, land and future. Second, get rid of any hazards that reasonable watchfulness can spot—ditches without crossovers, rusting equipment sitting around for children to cut themselves on, parking methods that expose anyone to being struck as they cross your lot or get into or out of their cars. It may seem unfair, but pick the upper branches of full-sized fruit trees before opening them to the picking public, removing everything beyond easy reach. Tempt no one to use nature's ladder, the tree.

Let no one use your expensive equipment—which could make you liable if they tumble—or use their own makeshifts. Another way is to open only heavy-bearing dwarf trees for public harvesting.

Planning. How do you plan a pick-it-yourself operation? Set up that full insurance coverage. Then decide what you will sell. Figure out when and where to advertise that you're ready to open field or orchard to bargain-conscious vegetable and fruit lovers. Which crops? When will they be at their peak? Line up the local newspaper and other sources of advertising space and time, putting out a preliminary announcement with an approximate date, then a final blockbuster when harvest time arrives.

Make up easily understandable rules for customers to see and follow. They need guidance for safe and easy harvesting and you need coverage against pirating and other troubles. What do you expect them to do to get the crops? If it's field crops the danger is low, but still they should know how to tell when things are perfectly ripe and what they shouldn't harvest for their own good. (Are you sure they'll know immature corn when they can't see the golden ear?)

NO CLIMBING.

PICK IN MARKED AREAS ONLY.

HARVEST ONLY AS MUCH AS YOU CAN COMFORTABLY CARRY—YOU CAN COME BACK FOR MORE.

IF YOU CAN'T REACH IT FROM THE GROUND IT ISN'T YOURS.

ONCE IT'S PICKED IT'S YOURS TO PAY FOR. IF IN DOUBT, ASK SUPERVISOR.

Managing. Get yourself enough dependable supervisors—your biggest labor cost—to be sure customers, crop, and your profits will be safe. One kindly soul sitting at the entrance isn't going to be able to watch, guide, and help everyone unless you've opened only a tiny area to the public.

Assign one or a few people, clearly identified by clothes or armband, to a field with low-growing crops. Where visibility is good one or two people can handle everything, but for tree crops you should have at least one employee for every dozen people picking, simply because it's harder to see the people for the trees. For an orchard, providing a walkie talkie for each attendant is a handy precaution for both safety and good management. The public may be doing the picking, but that doesn't free you of responsibility.

Turnover may be slow, with some people wanting to spend the whole day doing a leisurely job—it's not as if they were hired for the job, though they may put in as many hours as professional pickers, and some may do as good a job, meaning they'll end the day with a good harvest—for themselves and for you.

Plan plenty of parking spaces off the road and away from the picking area. You'll need safe, restricted entrances and exits, and on a busy day a parking attendant will reduce confusion and make everything safer. For a good-sized crop of a favorite fruit or vegetable, figure that you can park 100 cars on each acre of space that's suitable for parking. Only experience will tell just how much space you'll fill. Put the cars on dense sod to keep people from getting stuck or covering themselves and their cars with muck in wet seasons.

Containers. What shall they carry the produce in? Probably it's better for you to supply and charge for containers in spite of the expense, because that way both you and customers will know exactly how much they're picking and buying. An assortment of boxes and crates and bags makes measuring and weighing confusing. Sell standard-sized pint, quart, peck, or bushel boxes or cartons. Plan to weigh the smaller items like berries so that you won't have arguments about how full the containers are. That also will save handling, important because emptying the boxes onto scales and back again will damage fruit. Set the scale for the amount the box weighs to give the net weight.

For bigger things like apples, peaches, and vegetables, also have customers use your containers. Plastic bags with drawstrings, Blakeley suggests, will give accurate measuring and make convenient carriers. They'll save you from having to weigh the goods, which absorbs time, too. Of course you can't just give the containers away; people should pay for them as they check in and get your rules and instructions.

Customer flow. Be sure you plan how customers should flow from parking area to picking area, and plan to make them stick to the specified paths. First, advertise precisely when they should come and go. Have signs telling them how to get to the picking area and where to park. An attendant is a help in getting them where you want them and telling them how to get there. They can check in at your market if it's close enough to the fields or orchards. Once inside the market, they are exposed to everything you have to sell, though they may not be interested in anything but the crop they came for. If the parking area and market are far from the picking grounds, you may have to transport the pickers both ways. The best, some people say, is a farm wagon pulled by horse or tractor, making the ride an adventure in itself. People may not mind a short hike if the way is pleasant and not in full sun, but anything more than a hundred or so yards gets discouraging, at least at the end of a long hot day's harvesting.

Water and toilets. People also need some kind of refreshment. That may not mean another source of income for you, because most will bring their own drinkables and lunches. But you should have water that they can get at, either from handy faucets or a tank on a truck or wagon. Shaded areas set aside for resting will be welcome. And sanitary toilets can't be done without. The kind you rent with regular emptying service are a real convenience. Johnny on the Spot and others are listed in phone books almost everywhere.

Chapter 10

All the Answers

You probably didn't count on finding the answer to every question about roadside marketing in this book. But I know who *can* give you the answers to almost anything—the roadside marketers themselves, and not just nearby neighbors, helpful as they may be.

WHO KNOWS MARKETS
BETTER THAN MARKETERS?

If you feel you're running short of ideas, find out about the marketers' meetings held every year in most states. Extension services put them on as another aid for farmers and marketers. They are well attended by people who share their problems and solutions. Helpful colleagues and friendly competitors give prepared talks and run discussions. Seminars, round-table discussions, question-and-answer talks, and plain bull sessions will freshen your ideas and reduce your troubles, or at least show you they're not yours alone. Your county agent can tell you when they will be held in your own state and in others nearby.

You can also write to extension services in other states for printed-up summaries or minutes that record the sessions, if you can't get there to ask the questions that interest you most, or if you want to read up on earlier meetings. The cost for these minutes is very low for the wealth of information you can mine from them.

No need to worry about giving away prized ideas that will make the competition healthier than you. Ideas are so easy to copy that it's silly to be over-protective. Besides, as I've said, no two markets are alike, however hard an operator tries to copy. And people in this business are notorious for cooperating as well as competing. There is more than enough public to go around, almost everywhere.

ASSOCIATE WITH THE BEST

Other sources of information you can't afford to ignore are the associations of roadside marketers that many states have. Probably the best place to go for news of these is your Farm Bureau. They can give you names and addresses and tell you what the associations have done or mean to do.

In *American Vegetable Grower* (June, 1973) M. E. Cravens says that where no marketer alone can dent business in a big metropolitan area, together a group can advertise and promote themselves into a share of the money that's spent on produce. Working together, all can spend their money wisely, and all can expand their businesses if they plan things right. One of the associations' best contributions is making more varieties of produce available to all members, swapping or selling specialties among themselves.

The first such associations were set up to do something about the roadside hucksters masquerading as farmers but selling inferior merchandise by deceptive advertising. The earliest association wrote itself standards that would work well today, more than 50 years later. They set up qualifications for cleanliness, quality, and integrity, and allowed no one into the association who didn't meet the specifications. Groups then and since usually have designed themselves an easy-to-spot symbol that all members display as proof that they live up to their ideal of serving the public's interest in quality and integrity. Jersey Standard Certified Markets even decided to display at every market an emblem recognizable to anyone and from a distance—a working windmill that could pump the market's water.

STAFF INSPECTION

These associations have committees that try to inspect every member market periodically to see to it that the standards for products, advertising and merchandising are all served.

Some have printed forms that get members to hand around information and ideas, with the praiseworthy aim of keeping every market successful. They can also get together on purchasing supplies for their markets, seeking the advantage that centralized buying gives. They cooperate on everything from sharing produce they can't or won't grow for themselves to bags and containers with the association's emblem printed on them. Anything that they buy in bulk, of course, gives them good savings for all. Other things add to their cooperative advantages: shared promotional materials and shipping in merchandise from a distance (because bulk freight rates are better).

TRAIN FOR COMPETENCE

Some associations hold annual training clinics, hiring or volunteering people to teach the kind of salesmanship all prefer to see, as well as how to handle money, pricing, procuring supplies, and the other matters that all agree they need to know more about. Together, they can get coverage on radio and television and in newspapers much more effectively and cheaply than they could one by one. Hospitalization bought at group rates helps everyone, too. Groups are also better at handling added labor that's needed at busy seasons, plus accounting services and life and casualty group insurance. These are not the only reasons, but they might convince even the most rugged individualist that being a joiner sometimes pays off.

WHAT EVER HAPPENED TO THE FARMERS' MARKET?

Another way of cooperating and of building business is the farmers' market. It is a way of cooperating on marketing facilities in or near a city, where everyone pays a fee for space in an inside or outside market at a central place that can attract very large numbers of people. All can sell directly to the public there instead of or in addition to the market on the farm.

Markets like this were more appealing in the past, but they seem to be coming back. In 1974, Iowa Representative Ed Mezvinsky was spurring attempts to set up farmers' markets across the nation as an antidote to endlessly spiraling food prices. He had a "Food Action Arm" staff working with Department of Agriculture officials in Washington to put together policies that would encourage people to set up such markets.

MARKETING TOGETHER

What *is* a farmers' market, really? Very simply it is a kind of organized marketing, and like roadside marketing, this market gets producers and consumers together, to benefit both. A long time ago farmers set up retailing facilities in the cities where they could share the expenses and have a much bigger audience than they could ever gather alone out in the country. Most big cities had farmers' markets or something like them way back through history. And an arrangement this sound certainly is as practical today.

Boston has the New England Produce Center, Boston Market Terminal in Chelsea, a huge affair that gathers food shipped by railroad, truck, and plane, and from nearby producers, all in one huge, constantly expanding complex. Large markets like this one sell mostly to retailers. One of the best reasons for the farmers' market is that the people can get better and varied produce without traveling to several and more distant producing regions.

Canadian markets. Canada seems to have gone further toward bringing back the farmers' market, according to Thomas A. Bennett of Agriculture Canada, writing in *Canadian Farm Economics* (vol. 9, no. 5). They've settled on three kinds. In the first, the marketers sell to consumers only; another has operators selling at wholesale only; and in the third kind, one market is used by both wholesalers and direct marketers, clearly separated from each other. Still others split their time and sell both ways. Each operator rents a stall, selling produce from either a stand or a truck. Farmers spend all kinds of hours and days in the markets, some of them taking part in selling at more than one market.

These markets have caught on so well that Canada now has 119 of them, concentrated mostly in the more important crop-producing provinces. British Columbia has only three, perhaps because so many of its producers sell at roadside markets, making about $6 million in such sales annually. Ontario, though, has half the country's farmers' markets, with some old and outstanding ones. The Kitchener Market has been running since 1830 and re-opened in June 1974 with $3 million worth of market and parking space. It has 124 inside vendors of everything from vegetables to meat, plus 84 outside sellers of fruit and vegetables. Of the produce marketers, 25 or 30 sell only their own produce, the rest supplementing their sales with produce bought outside. The peak selling period runs from June to Thanksgiving, with Saturday sales in 1974 above $225,000.

Why the comeback? Mr. Bennett, talking of other successful markets in Ontario, says that nostalgia is not the only power behind the renewed Canadian interest in farmers' markets. Some set up in shopping centers have awakened downtown merchants to their drawing possibilities.

Consumers are interested, partly because of the "back to nature" movement. But the producers are less eager, says Mr. Bennett, because the markets take plenty of labor, cost a lot, and swallow much of the growers' time. The farmers do realize, though, that these markets are exposed to many people, and may cut down on the number of hours the operator has to keep his roadside market open (which can be handled by family labor), and together bring more of the customer's dollar to the farmer. The farmers' markets appeal most to producers who want to get into retailing, but whose operations are not well placed for roadside selling.

WHAT DOES A FARMERS' MARKET NEED?

Melvin W. Smith and M. E. Cravens put together a list of questions in 1963 for groups interested in organizing farmers' markets:

(1) Is a good volume of fresh fruits and vegetables available within 30 to 50 miles?

(2) Can you get three or four growers together who are interested in growing each major item of produce?

(3) Do you have 10 or 15 more producers who grow all other products, including fruit, vegetables, and flowers? These make a healthy market atmosphere.

(4) Are the producers willing to diversify what they produce?

(5) Can you find adequate market facilities at reasonable rates, and can they be securely financed?

(6) Does the market facility have adequate parking?

(7) Does the parking area have easy access to and from traffic?

Inside Marshall's, the displays are well-stocked and easy to reach.

(8) Do the marketers know enough about designing an adequate physical layout?

(9) Are the right kinds of customers nearby?

(10) Are there 25,000 to 100,000 families within a five-mile radius of the facility?

(11) Do the organizers know which hours and days would be best for marketing?

(12) Are enough of the people interested in financing the market so that it will be controlled by bona fide producers?

With all these questions answered to everyone's satisfaction, you should be able to start a working farmers' market to supplement the income you pull in back by the edge of the road.

Appendix

Like to Read More?

For the reader who wants more, there are many very useful publications available from state university extension services. A few articles are also in print in popular journals.

The first of these is Roger G. Ginder, who writes *Roadside Market News,* issued by the Cooperative Extension Service, University of Delaware, Newark, Delaware 19711. Mr. Ginder gathers and compiles great quantities of information for marketers. His work is most specifically for people in his state, yet his information is widely usable, and I recommend his publications to you. I have cited selected material from his newsletters of June 1970 to June, 1973.

A well of information is Purdue University, where until recently Ransom A. Blakeley, Associate Professor and Marketing Specialist, wrote *Indiana Farm Market News,* distributed by Indiana Extension Service, Purdue University, West Lafayette, Indiana 47907. Mr. Blakeley was a prolific purveyor of helpful printed matter from speeches he and others gave, from transcribed conferences, and from his own newsletter. I am indebted to him for many fine publications from 1973 to June 1975. At several places in this book are samples of the material Purdue can supply.

The University of Maine has a few specifically serviceable publications, including a study by Homer B. Metzger, A.

Prysunka, F. French, and W. Erhardt on *Marketing Fresh Vegetables Through Roadside Stands,* published in August 1974, which is available from the Life Sciences Agriculture Experiment Station, University of Maine at Orono. The study was done back in 1973, but the conclusions the authors reached seem likely to hold for some time. Homer B. Metzger also studied "Fresh Marketing of Maine Lowbush Blueberries Through Retail Stores and Roadside Stands," a practical and well-planned booklet for a continuing publication series called "Research in the Life Sciences." The first part, dated May 1974, is "Market Acceptance of a Commercial Package," and the second, published in June 1974, is "Harvesting, Handling, Sales Volume, Costs and Returns."

R. Alden Miller, regional vegetable specialist, Cooperative Extension Service, University of Massachusetts, 36 Harvard Street, Worcester, Massachusetts 01608, supplied copies of his Northeast Region Vegetable Marketing Letter," which contains much current advice and good ideas.
current advice and good ideas.

Like many other specialists in roadside marketing, Lou Albano has his own market in Concord, Massachusetts. He is Consultant in Roadside Marketing for the Massachusetts Department of Agriculture, which distributes his "Clearing House, A Newsletter for Roadside Market Operators," a chatty publication meant to encourage marketers to improve their own businesses.

M. E. Cravens, professor in the Department of Agricultural Economics and Rural Sociology, Ohio State University, Columbus, Ohio 43210, has done much writing on this subject. "Roadside Marketing by Ohio Farmers" was published in *Ohio Report* 57 (5), pages 67-69 (September-October 1972). "Farm Marketing, California Style" was published in *American Vegetable Grower,* June, 1973.

Farm Roadside Marketing in Ontario is a 32-page illustrated introduction with a few ideas you won't find elsewhere. Robert Cobbledick, marketing specialist, Ontario Ministry of Agriculture and Food, Vineland Station, Ontario, Canada, kindly supplied this and other information about Canadian marketing. Ask for Publication 63.

You can learn about Canadian farmers' markets in Thomas A. Bennett's "Direct Marketing of Fresh Fruit and Vegetables: A Look at Farmers' Markets in Canada," published August 1974 in *Canadian Farm Economics,* volume 9, number 3. Mr. Bennett is head of the Agricultural and Special Crops Section, Marketing and Trade Division, Economics Branch, Agriculture Canada, Ottawa, Ontario.

An informative article telling how well some people do with their roadside markets was written by M. C. Goldman. His "Farm Stands That Deliver Customers" appeared in *Organic Gardening and Farming,* October 1972. Joseph F. Hauck, extension and research specialist in marketing at the New Jersey Agricultural Experiment Station, Rutgers University, New Brunswick, New Jersey, did a small booklet some time ago called "Roadside Marketing in the Garden State."

Gene Logsdon reported in "A Plum Nutty Way to Profit" *(Farm Journal* 96:51, March 1972) how two farm wives showed their husbands they could make extra money retailing specialty jams and jellies in a roadside market. And he told about "Your Best Cash Crops" in *Organic Gardening and Farming,* August 1973, suggesting how some crops can bring both small and large growers a profit, but other crops can ruin them. He tells how to know which are best bets.

Silas B. Weeks, extension economist of the Cooperative Extension Service, University of New Hampshire, Durham, New Hampshire, in August 1961 published a useful booklet titled "Managing the Roadside Farm Stand for Profit." Norman F. Whippen, associate marketing specialist, with the same organization, wrote "Roadside Selling in New Hampshire," Extension Bulletin 142, published in September 1957.

You may wonder if *reading* about roadside marketing can help the beginner and the established marketer. I believe that the two better ways of learning about it—experience and talking with people who have experience—are hard for many people to come by, and books can save time. Perhaps in some corner where I haven't looked are other, more recent publications to add to those mentioned here.

Index

Sale 2.40

Cash From Your Garden

Freshness, 64, 66–71
Fruit, 30; baskets, 168–72

Ginder, Roger, 70–71, 80, 83–85,
    91, 95, 118–21, 123, 155,
    173, 178, 200
Gourds, 178–79
Grading, 78
Greenhouse, 69, 166, 172–73, 175

Holly, 181
Honey, 165

Ice, 69-71
Impulse buying, 97-98
Insurance, 123–30, 189–90, 195
Inventory, 64–65; records, 108

Landscaping of market, 59, 174
Legal considerations, 35–36
Lighting, 45
Logotype, 138, 156

Maintenance, 58–59; of outdoor
    signs, 139
Managing a market, 53–87;
    checklist, 60–63
Market, layout, 40–47, 153–56;
    location, 31–35; size, 10–12,
    37–40
Markup, 80–83, 86; conversion,
    84 (table)
Miller, R. Alden, 117–18, 139,
    161–63, 185, 201
Moisture conditioning, 68–69
Money handling, 102, 117–22
Mulches, 176–77

Nursery stock, 172–77, 180

Orchards, 189–91

Organic gardening, 167–68

Packaging, 78–79, 156–60
Pallet box, 159
Parking, 45–47, 190–92
Pest control, 75–77, 158
"Pick-your-own" sales, 28,
    186–92
Plants, for sale, 166–67, 172–76
Preserves, 165
Pricing, 79–87
Produce, quality control, 72–74
    (table)
Profit and loss statement, 108,
    111–14
Profit margin, 83
Profits, 1–6; increase of, 120–22,
    161-92; table, 121

Quick sale display, 65–66, 71, 78

Refrigerated storage area, 42
Refrigeration, 69–71, 153
Restrooms, 58, 182, 192
Rhododendrons, 181
Root cellar, 70

Sales slips, 101–102
Seedlings, 176
Selling, 96–104; schedule, 48–49
Spoilage records, 108
Stevens, Robert, 172–77, 179–81
Surplus, buying, 3–4; selling, 2–3

Taxes, 5, 58–59, 122–23
Terrariums, 179–80
Tomatoes, 68, 166
Tote tray, 159–60
Type of structure, 38–40

Zoning, 35, 137